Teachable Moments

Teachable Moments

Tales of Triumph and Lessons Gone Awry

Dennis M. Fare and Allison Coyle

ROWMAN & LITTLEFIELD
Lanham • Boulder • New York • London

Published by Rowman & Littlefield
A wholly owned subsidiary of The Rowman & Littlefield Publishing Group, Inc.
4501 Forbes Boulevard, Suite 200, Lanham, Maryland 20706
www.rowman.com

Unit A, Whitacre Mews, 26-34 Stannary Street, London SE11 4AB

Copyright © 2017 by Dennis M. Fare and Allison Coyle

All rights reserved. No part of this book may be reproduced in any form or by any electronic or mechanical means, including information storage and retrieval systems, without written permission from the publisher, except by a reviewer who may quote passages in a review.

British Library Cataloguing in Publication Information Available

Library of Congress Cataloging-in-Publication Data

Title: Teachable moments: Tales of triumph and lessons gone awry / Dennis M. Fare and Allison Coyle.
Description: Lanham : Rowman & Littlefield, 2017.
ISBN 9781475828245 (cloth : alkaline paper) | ISBN 9781475828252 (paper : alkaline paper) | ISBN 9781475828269 (electronic)

∞ ™ The paper used in this publication meets the minimum requirements of American National Standard for Information Sciences Permanence of Paper for Printed Library Materials, ANSI/NISO Z39.48-1992.

Printed in the United States of America

This book is dedicated to all the friends and family who heard about our best and worst days at school—listening to all of the most highlighted lessons, as well as the most catastrophic moments of our teaching careers.

For your advice and your care, these pages are also dedicated to those mentors along the way. Without college professors who kept in touch, without our own teachers who inspired us in our teaching paths, without colleagues who shared in an understanding of the inner-workings of what we do every day, all of these ups and downs would never be possible.

This book is dedicated to the morning bell, to recess, and to those specific days that we will never forget for the rest of our lives. This book is dedicated to the not-being-able-to-sleep toss-and-turn on the night before the first day of school, even after all these years.

Most of all, though, this text is dedicated to our students—those who have taught us more lessons about ourselves than any book ever could. To those students who worked hard, to those students who gave us grief, to those students with which we failed to connect, and to those whose faces remain etched in our memory—we thank you.

Contents

Preface: A Note about Teaching ... ix
   Dennis M. Fare

Introduction ... xi
   A Note from a Teacher: Allison Coyle ... xii
   A Note from a School Administrator: Dennis M. Fare ... xiii

1 Planning and Preparation ... 1
   "On the Ride to Work" ... 2
   "Dig Your Roots" ... 3
   "Vobackulary" ... 6
   "America Under Attack" ... 8
   "Two for Timer" ... 10
   "I Don't Judge Them by Their Skin Color" ... 13
   "Multiple-Choice" ... 15

2 The Classroom Environment ... 17
   "Somewhere in the Middle" ... 18
   "I Have No Mouth and I Must Scream" ... 20
   "6:00 P.M." ... 23
   "Stephen" ... 23
   "A Change in Plans" ... 27
   "Character Degradation" ... 29
   "Quicksand" ... 31
   "Myth Busters" ... 33
   "Something Different" ... 35

3 Instruction ... 37
   "The First Six Weeks" ... 38
   "Intermission" ... 41
   "Balancing Act" ... 43
   "Columbine" ... 45
   "You're Going to Have to Produce Data" ... 47
   "All but One" ... 49
   "More Than a Few Seconds" ... 51

4 Professional Responsibilities ... 53
   "Re: Re: Re: Re:" ... 55
   "Change That" ... 57
   "To Whom It May Concern" ... 60

"Mass Destruction"	62
"Secret Keepers"	65
"A True Honor"	67
"Cheese Sandwiches"	68
"The Expert in Anything was Once a Beginner"	70
"Hashtags and Friend Requests"	72
"Beware the Ides of March"	74
Final Thoughts	79
Final Words from a Teacher . . .	79
Final Words from a School Administrator . . .	79
About the Authors	81

Preface

A Note about Teaching

Dennis M. Fare

I once had a college professor in my graduate program. Her name was Dr. Lesliee Antonette.

In this course, Dr. Antonette was viewed as the type of teacher with specific expectations and high standards. If you checked any of the online professor-rating systems, Dr. Antonette was characterized as pretty tough.

We learned about multicultural literature and how to make those pages come to life in our future classrooms.

Many books and many classrooms later, and Dr. Antonette's lessons still remain.

Part of the course requirements was to respond personally to each of the multicultural texts that we would read for assignments. Dr. Antonette referred to these as "multicultural response paradigms." Something about the text could/would/should have been worthy of response, either through its content or the way the content was communicated to the reader.

I have to say, the assignment itself, while not overbearing, served as a powerful tool to Dr. Antonette, as the professor and to me as the student.

This opened up a trusting conduit through which to communicate on paper, where we would synthesize our thoughts, and Dr. Antonette would always respond in her own personal, distinct handwriting.

On the last assignment of the semester, my written response was particularly reflective, almost revealing. I remember being nervous to hand in my work.

Dr. Antonette actually asked me to come to her office and handed my paper back. At the bottom was her penmanship: *Follow your passion, and the world will take care of itself.*

Our conversation itself is blurred in my memory, but her handwriting still sits in a folder in my office desk.

Her effort, those words, *the time*—all of it mattered more than any textbook, any written page, any planned lesson could have taught me.

Remember that those subtle interactions with our students will mean more and will last longer than any unit in any prescribed curriculum ever could.

Introduction

Quite purposefully, this book is written through two very separate lenses, and the stories presented to you are told through two distinct voices. Listen to each carefully. In reviewing various teacher-evaluation tools and frameworks, we have learned that each is constructed based on four different principles: planning and preparation, classroom environment, instruction, and professional responsibilities. Each attempts to define what we do as educators, and through this attempt, you are evaluated by reviewing the various traits and components that make up each category.

Consider this collection of essays a reflection of sorts—a series of perspectives that introduce the many layers that showcase the vocation of teaching. As we look from a new(er) bird's-eye view, our goal is to observe and study the nuances of what makes the life of a teacher so multilayered. The perspectives found in this book will be through the lens of a current administrator, as well as a new teacher. The purpose here is to look at how we balance our role as a new educator, looking closely at an administrator's expectations with that of the realities of the new-teacher experience.

The way one starts in our profession is quite similar to that of ourselves as students. This idea of being a part of a community—whether that community is elementary or secondary in nature—seems vital, and our interactions with parents, colleagues, administrators, and students can make all the difference in these experiences. As you read through, you will find that it is in the details that you will notice common threads among the stories. The ultimate purpose here is to both reflect and understand the value of this reflection as we look at practices and relationship building through a variety of scenarios.

Through each anecdote, think specifically about the various lessons that exist as the new teacher experiences interactions with students, fellow colleagues, and the classroom and school-wide culture.

Use these classroom visits as a practical guide to teaching—the real stuff you do not learn from the education textbook but, rather, the lessons you learn once you begin in the reality inside your very own classroom. Try your best, at times, to put educational theory into practice—or if you have to, put the theoretical perspective aside every now and then and follow your gut.

Before we look inside some real classrooms, it is important to ensure the following: During your first year, it is critical to remind yourselves why you started in this profession in the first place. While this ideal should not be extinguished through reading these anecdotes, it is imperative that you also balance this passion for your careers with the very realistic worlds that are contained within the confines of the four walls of your very own classrooms.

While it is exciting, teaching is *hard*.

This book was designed to help you find your way.

A NOTE FROM A TEACHER: ALLISON COYLE

A fellow teacher and friend of mine recently announced to a group of our peers, "Teaching made a list for top ten most stressful jobs." Before the words even left her lips, a series of eye-rolling, scoffing, and blatantly sardonic, "Yeah, okays," ensued from her audience of accountants, other business professionals, and even a marine biologist.

"Did 'clown' make the list, too?" asked Accountant, to which the crowd went wild with guffaws and high-fives.

I nodded in support of my friend, Stephanie, and said, simply, "I believe it!"

And, I get it. What makes a teacher worthy of a list, which boasts the likes of police officers, firefighters, pilots, and army generals? Well, we asked our friends these questions: How many decisions do you make on the job? How often do you turn down time with your loved ones for your job? How often do you plan for your week ahead? How often do you reflect on the work you do? How many people are you responsible for at work? How many times have you *cried* on the job? And not just self-pitying tears because you are tired, but tears because the work you do matters and it impacts vulnerable, impressionable people?

To assuage their two increasingly aggravated peers, our business-world counterparts backed down.

"Okay, I was kidding about the circus comparison," Accountant conceded.

As I reflect on the realities of first-year teaching, the above conversation feels like an important starting point. As a teacher, it is necessary to understand, and to gently forgive, the naïveté of those outside of the teaching realm. Until you are a part of the profession, you cannot begin to understand the subtleties that even a single day in the classroom holds.

Like many of you reading this book, my journey began as an enthusiastic undergraduate, pursuing an education degree. For four years, I refined my knowledge of English literature, of writing standards, of best practices. I learned the latest ways to teach others to read, to write, to explore their thoughts. The quintessential idealist, I entered the teaching profession believing that imparting my own knowledge would be simple, that I would look back on the experiences that earned me a degree in English literature and adolescent education and easily and effectively impart that knowledge unto others. After my first week of student teaching in an inner-city high school, a guidance counselor (whom I visited for myself, not for a student) looked at me with concern and asked, "What? Did you think you'd be teaching grammar and writing here? Girl, just worry about gaining respect."

Initially, the news that my life was not going to be all *Gatsby* and creative writing destroyed me. That bit of tough love, though, taught me something no textbook ever could. I held this first lesson close to me as I embarked on my first year as a high school teacher in a different district a few months later. Student teaching had forced me to *let go* of my expectations, and my first year of teaching confirmed that malleability is everything.

This book reveals many of those learning experiences, as well as some of the most rewarding moments of first-year teaching, through anecdotes that reflect the different aspects of our profession. Firsthand experiences are, truly, the best way to impart the reality of teaching unto those who have yet to have the privilege to experience it for themselves.

You will find that among the chaos, the unannounced observations, the skipped lunches, the deserved title of "top stressful job," is a profession unlike any other. I was always told that teaching would be rewarding. And it is.

The nature of the rewards, I guess, is what has really been eye-opening for me. Honestly, teaching is a profession made up of moments that, consistently, make you believe in the good of people, in the possibility for growth, and in the utter magic of human connection.

A NOTE FROM A SCHOOL ADMINISTRATOR: DENNIS M. FARE

It is understandable to be excited about your first classroom. What you will experience in setting up your own space, in sitting down to prepare lessons, and the night before you really start is extremely difficult to encapsulate in words—and *we get that*.

But this is our attempt to do so.

When I walk into a classroom, I never expect for it to be perfect; in fact, I know that all teachers—even master teachers—always have room to improve, as is the case with all school administrators and leaders. Many of us, though, are designed to yearn for perfection. The perfect procedures, the perfect student behavior, the perfect execution of a lesson—especially when someone in a suit is watching us from the sidelines.

Now, all of this is more high stakes than ever before. The way in which we document a lesson has vastly evolved, as we gather information in greater detail, and our post-observation conferences are required to be more thoughtful. This shift in responsibility and expectation, while something that should be celebrated, is, *too*, a challenge.

While I recognize that having an administrator in the classroom is, at times, an intimidating experience, I have to remind you of the reason why we are there. First, many of us miss the classroom, and observing gives us that instructional piece that we have loved from the beginning. Second, this evaluation and appraisal of your lesson is important in your supervision in being better at our craft. It is important to reframe the way you think about this process, as it is a necessary reality in your professional duty in working toward ever honing your work as a classroom teacher.

As you move through the classroom hallways of this book, stop and reflect on what you will do, and in visiting each of these classrooms, think about how you might have approached these scenarios differently. Last, decide how and if your different approach was either better or worse than the one presented.

In our everyday practices inside the classroom, we have a multitude of responsibilities—each expected to be executed with precision. At times, we falter, and *that is okay*. Decide here which of those mistakes are forgivable and rectifiable and which are not.

Along the way, enjoy your observations, and pay attention to the details; after all, being a better teacher means being mindful to separate each piece that makes our profession so very complicated and intriguing, and make conscious strides at being better—*in any way that you can.*

ONE
Planning and Preparation

In what a former supervisor called a "house-keeping" department meeting, one of Ms. Diaz's colleagues raised her hand, looked around, and asked, "Does everyone keep two sets of lesson plans and when one plan doesn't work out fully, do you go with the other?" Another colleague responded, "Yeah, and I make sure I have a physical copy of the plans and a digital copy."

"Suck-ups," thought Ms. Diaz as she sat quietly.

Of course, at the time, she always did have *a* plan. But to have two and to keep multiple copies just seemed like an utter waste of time. That was one of the first department meetings Ms. Diaz ever attended. Naïveté had filled her with hubris.

It did not take long for Ms. Diaz to realize the necessity of her peers' seemingly ludicrous overplanning.

Ms. Diaz remembered her colleagues' double-plan confession when a lesson of hers, for which she had allotted 55 minutes, actually took 20. Students read independently for the remainder of the time, but at the end of the period, she really felt as though she had wasted 35 valuable minutes. It was not the last time Ms. Diaz would mistime a lesson, and even some of her most experienced peers have admitted that, sometimes, activities just do not go as planned. By the end of her first year of teaching, she could have been one of the people nodding along to the question, "Does everyone keep two sets of lesson plans?"

When teachers and school administrators think about the framework of education, planning and preparation stand out clearly as the two most foundational supports. Whether you are a kindergarten teacher or a college professor, planning and preparing need to be the two guiding forces of your career. Within these two categories is everything from knowing the diverse population of students for whom you are responsible, designing lessons and assessments, and understanding, fully, expertly, the content you deliver.

Teachers are allotted preparatory time every day. Sometimes prep periods, though, tempt teachers to take a mental break—to do something unrelated to the classroom, and occasionally, that personal time is really necessary. However, do everything you can to stay on track and focused during that time. The more you plan during those apportioned periods, the less stress you will experience outside of the workplace and the less likely you will desperately find yourself with 35 precious minutes to fill.

"ON THE RIDE TO WORK"

It was particularly snowy on that January morning. Ms. Rizzo expected a snow day, but to her chagrin, the school schedule was as regular as any other day.

Ms. Rizzo's lesson plan consisted of follow-up work related to polynomials. In all honesty, she wasn't particularly excited.

With the lack of time this week, Ms. Rizzo was not able to adequately prepare materials to help students in their independent practice, so Ms. Rizzo looked to center most of this lesson on direct instruction. And that was okay. According to Ms. Rizzo, there was a time and place for direct instruction.

Time and place: (1) when you have to introduce new material to students and (2) when you don't have the time to prepare anything for students' activities.

The entire commute to school, Ms. Rizzo toggled among three tasks: avoiding black ice on the road, appropriately changing the radio station when a commercial would emerge, and thinking of ideas that would make the impending lesson a better one.

She felt almost panicked because she was not necessarily in the mood to face a group of unaffected young teenagers.

Ms. Rizzo got to the point of supreme concentration—the type where you think so hard that you forget about the song on the radio, and when you eventually refocus, you realize that you're well into the radio infomercials.

Reminding herself that she submitted her lesson plans already, she knew she had a back-up plan. And that back-up plan was direct instruction.

The kids sit there, notebooks open, scribbling the necessary formulas and mathematical steps. It would be fine. *Really, the kids will be okay.*

Ms. Rizzo still continued scouring the unused recesses of her brain for some ideas. In her quest to find some semblance of a notion that had a flake of originality beyond that of a lesson-plan Google search, she thought of *something*.

Students would use colored blocks and construction paper to work through different polynomial operations. Ms. Rizzo remembered that she had materials in the bottom of her classroom desk.

Good thing she got to work early.

The parking lot looked abnormally empty, probably because Ms. Rizzo's fellow teachers were busy avoiding the same patches of black ice on the road on this cold winter morning. The snow plows were just beginning to sweep the blanket of white fluff from the black pavement. The crisp lines of each numbered spot began to appear. With each turn of the snow plow, more and more of the school's parking-spot numbers appeared.

Ms. Rizzo loved numbers so much. She counted the prime numbers as they slowly presented themselves in the frosty morning hue.

From her classroom window, she could see the snow slowly dissipate as she carefully laid out graphing calculators atop each student desk in rows. Colored blocks were neatly arranged at the front of the classroom.

Ms. Rizzo loved numbers, but loved teaching even more.

Sometimes, just sometimes, the best-laid plans are those that happen when you're right about to turn into the parking lot.

Reflection/Discussion Questions

1. What about this anecdote should be celebrated most with regard to Ms. Rizzo as a teacher? What are some of the pitfalls in her approaches?
2. We often draft our lesson plans for the entire week. Things happen, and lesson plans shift. What might be a sound rationale for making such switches? At what point should changing a lesson be discouraged?
3. In making the adjustments that Ms. Rizzo did, how do you anticipate Ms. Rizzo's students responding differently to these changes?

"DIG YOUR ROOTS"

Mr. Connor's fifth-grade class quickly became famous for many reasons—for the way Mr. Connor was known to catch a student doodling and, instead of taking away the drawing, complete the doodle; for the motivational chants he led that would sometimes echo out into the hallway; for the joy on his students' faces when they departed from his classroom each day. In just his second year of teaching, he had even created a history project that captivated students and, quite honestly, evoked a bit of jealousy from some of the more seasoned, traditional teachers.

"This project is called, 'Dig your Roots!'" Mr. Connor announced as he opened up a projected slide of a lengthy family tree, the middle of which displayed a picture of Mr. Connor with his tongue sticking out.

He had their attention. Giggles erupted around the room, and hands shot up, little voices with big questions waited to be heard.

Mr. Connor handed out rubrics and guidelines and then verbally discussed the requirements while students followed along on their handouts.

"You are going to use the online resources provided to trace your ancestry as far back as George Washington." Gasps.

"Or at least to the Cold War." Students had just learned about this time period, and felt proud to put the year to the historic event.

"In addition to providing a nice visual of your family tree, you also need to be ready to party! Each one of you will bring in a dish indicative of your heritage. You'll be digging your roots and *eating* your roots."

Students began turning to one another in excitement. "I'll probably have my mom make these really good little meatball things that she always makes for parties."

"My mom makes baklava, and it's so good. I'll definitely bring that."

One boy, Michael, turned to his friend, Veronica, and asked, excitedly, "What are you going to bring, Veronica?"

"Uh, I don't know yet. I need to ask my parents what they think," Veronica responded, trying to disguise her complete discomfort.

When the bell rang, Veronica was visibly relieved. Mr. Connor, surprised that his star pupil seemed unenthused, made a mental note to keep an eye on her the next day.

And when the next day came, students had already, clearly, begun their research.

"Mr. Connor, one of my ancestors was a Nordic Viking!"

Mr. Connor nodded encouragingly, all the while thinking, "Oh my, not actually something to be proud of."

"Mr. Connor, my grandmother came all the way here from Africa — on a boat!"

While Mr. Connor welled with a bit of pride at the genuine elation that encapsulated the room, his concerns for Veronica became ever increasing. While other students spent their computer lab time tinkering away on the prepaid Ancestry.com site or looking up recipes, Veronica remained on her student portal, absentmindedly checking her other homework assignments.

"Veronica, can I talk to you for a second in the hallway?"

A teacher, in this manner, had never before approached Veronica, and her nerves were evident.

"Uh, sure," Veronica stammered as she rose from her seat to slink, a bit shamefully, into the hallway.

"How come you're not using your lab time for the project, Veronica? Are you very busy with some of your other subjects?" Mr. Connor gently probed for the truth.

"No, I just," Veronica looked down at her feet, "I just don't know where to look."

"Well, we have a few programs provided by the school for this project. I can help you take a look when we go back inside."

"No, Mr. Connor," Veronica remained steady in her downward gaze, "My mom's family is from Italy and my dad's family is from Ireland. And my mom makes a lot of good Italian food and for St. Patrick's Day, she even makes corned beef and cabbage."

Mr. Connor nodded, thinking, "Okay, this all sounds fine."

"But I don't know if I should look at that family tree or at the one from Kazakhstan, where I was born. But I don't even know that mom's name and I don't know what they eat there and I don't think I can answer any questions on that country when I present my project."

Mr. Connor held back the guilt-ridden tears that threatened the back of his throat as he saw the first few droplets hit Veronica's Sketchers.

"Veronica, you are actually in such a wonderfully unique position," Mr. Connor managed, "Most people only have one family tree, but you might be able to have even more. And talk about culture! My goodness, you can research some of the traditions of all of these countries and talk about the many great places that make up who you are!"

Veronica's slumped shoulders softened a bit; she looked up and said, "You don't think it will be weird if I talk about having two different kinds of families? I don't think everyone in class knows I'm adopted."

"No, Veronica, I think it would be wonderful! But you know what, why don't we talk to your parents, see how they feel, and decide from there?"

"Okay, can I go back to class now?" Veronica asked.

Mr. Connor, having never been in this situation, was unsure of what to do next. "Should I go to guidance?" he wondered. "Should I call her parents on my own?" "Should I have Veronica present when I do?" "Should I change this 'Dig Your Roots' Project?"

Mr. Connor felt conflicted, but proceeded to call Veronica's parents at the end of the school day. He was thankful when Veronica's very understanding mother was already aware of the situation. Mrs. C explained that she had also encouraged Veronica to explore whichever side of the family seemed more interesting. She let Mr. Connor know that Veronica's knowledge of her adoption was openly talked about at home, and that Veronica's fears were mostly fueled by what the other students might think.

Mr. Connor assured Mrs. C that students in the class were respectful of one another and could probably really use learning about different types of families. Mrs. C, thankful for the insights, decided to leave the ultimate decision up to Veronica.

Mr. Connor watched Veronica's progress on the project as the two-week time frame ticked by. He saw her draw the Italian flag with her colored pencils, but he also saw her researching away on Kazak recipes. His fears began to dissipate as he found himself impressed by her bravery and maturity in conquering this project.

On the day of the "Dig Your Roots" event, parents were invited to watch their children present on their ancestry and their different cultural traditions, and to eat foods from around the world. Mr. and Mrs. C sat in one corner of the room; they watched, nervously, proudly, from the back as Veronica began her presentation.

Reflection/Discussion Questions

1. How could Mr. Connor have been more prepared for a student potentially in Veronica's position?
2. Was Mr. Connor's response to Veronica sensitive and appropriate?
3. What actions should Mr. Connor have taken after he spoke to Veronica? Should Mr. Connor have handled the situation any differently?

"VOBACKULARY"

Mr. Vespa was the only male on staff in Frackford Elementary School. He was one of two third-grade teachers, and he sometimes felt out of place in the district. For this reason, he allowed himself some entitlement and freedom in his lesson planning. Mr. Vespa had just begun an educational-leadership program at a local college, and since that took up a great deal of his time, his lessons were not always his first priority. The students seemed happy, and the administration did not bother him, so Mr. Vespa saw nothing wrong with his usual routines.

Mr. Vespa *was* following several aspects of the curriculum. He made sure students were assigned the same grade-level vocabulary that the other third-grade teacher assigned. He would give students a list of words, tell them to use the computer to look them up, and they would have a couple of days to memorize the definitions.

Mr. Vespa would sit at his desk and do his graduate work while the students fussed on computers and wrote down the definitions of the words. Mr. Vespa never actually checked the student lists for accuracy, but he did usually give a quiz after each unit to make sure students knew the real definitions. If a student appeared to be off track, playing a computer game or simply typing nonsense in a Word document, Mr. Vespa would pretty much turn a blind eye.

His intentions were not bad, necessarily; he just felt he was still reaching the outcomes the curriculum provided: acquire higher-level vocabulary. "Check," Mr. Vespa would think.

Mr. Vespa had developed a game for students to play after they wrote down the definitions of the vocabulary words. He called it "Vobackulary" because one student would stand in front of a projected screen with his or her back to the screen. A vocabulary word would appear behind the student, and the rest of the class would shout the definition until the student guessed the projected word. That student could then call on the next person to come up to the front of the room.

The game would often become quite loud, and Mr. Vespa could barely hear the definition shouted, as twenty students would scream for the spotlight. It kept everyone busy, though, and Mr. Vespa was usually able to get a lot of work done while they played.

During one of these particularly rowdy sessions, a teacher in an adjacent room complained to the principal about the noise level in Mr. Vespa's room. The principal decided to make an unannounced visit.

When she walked in, all of the students were out of their seats, jumping, screaming gibberish at a frazzled-looking student at the front of the room. Mr. Vespa had his own back turned while he was typing up a graduate paper on one of the student computers. He did not notice the principal's entrance.

Ms. Audra pulled one student aside, and asked very gently, "So, can you tell me what activity this is?"

The student was still riled and moved his feet from side to side, "This is Vobackulary!"

"Oh, very nice, and why do you play Vobackulary?"

"I don't know! You scream and scream until someone guesses the right vocabulary word!"

Ms. Audra could tell that the student could not wait to get back in on the game. "Okay, thank you!"

Ms. Audra had no further questions.

As the students continued to play, she approached Mr. Vespa who was visibly startled.

"Mr. Vespa, I am all about learning games, but would you mind meeting with me later? I just want to know how this particular one helps you reach your learning outcomes."

Ms. Audra left the room.

Mr. Vespa shut down the game and moved on to a more traditional activity. The students' energy level, though, made it nearly impossible to transition away from the game.

Mr. Vespa met with Ms. Audra at the end of the day. She immediately asked which instructional outcome Mr. Vespa was working toward by playing that particular game.

"They're acquiring grade-level vocabulary," Mr. Vespa said confidently.

"But, are they?" Ms. Audra questioned, "I asked one of your students why they were playing, and he seemed to think it was just for fun."

Mr. Vespa did not have a response.

"You need to be more mindful in creating activities that actually lead students to a certain outcome. I will be checking in weekly to see your progress."

Mr. Vespa was irritated as he left Ms. Audra's office. However, the next day when the average grade on the vocabulary quiz was below 70 percent, he thought that her criticism might have some validity.

Reflection/Discussion Questions

1. How should Mr. Vespa create instructional activities, including learning games?
2. Is it appropriate for Mr. Vespa to work on graduate work while his students are under his instruction?
3. How can a teacher be sure that students are working toward a desired outcome?

"AMERICA UNDER ATTACK"

It's strange that our history textbooks now include parts from our past that we, ourselves, have endured within our lifetime.

Ms. Krueg stepped away from her podium, which she used for a sense of comfort and security and from which she usually explained course concepts to students. She removed the podium from the classroom that morning.

Ms. Krueg still remembers that day from years ago—and the headlines that soon followed.

Two airplanes streaming through the sky, with a trail of white smoke—and *crash*. There it was. The most devastating day ever witnessed by Ms. Krueg.

She lived in New York City at the time, and incidentally, not too far from the World Trade Center; every now and then, Ms. Krueg would make a visit to the downtown area just to see how it had risen from its rubble.

But, as Ms. Krueg often admitted, it was not nearly the same now.

At nighttime, the downtown area surrounding the World Trade Center would feel like a barren dessert. The quiet and the still pocket of this distinct area was almost uncomfortable on the island of Manhattan. Perhaps, though, this stillness could be attributed to an appropriate memoriam. A moment of silence that lasted much longer than *just* a moment.

For the majority of her students, Ms. Krueg was not only shocked, but even more, disappointed, by the fact that they were not familiar with the more contemporary pages of their history textbooks. The 9/11 tragedy was nothing more than a forgotten memory—a forgotten memory that lingered with Ms. Krueg every single morning she would wake in the month of September.

The bodies plunging from the sky. The disarray of the city streets. She remembers the soot on the faces of those escaping for their lives in their business suits.

The fire alarms. The screeching of neighboring brick buildings.

The abandoned cars on the streets, soon covered by gray chunks of falling rock and body parts.

One image that remains with Ms. Krueg was what she perceived to be a businesswoman, in her appropriate navy blue dress suit, clutching onto what seemed to be a stranger. Both sobbing in confusion and covered in a layer of dust, as office paperwork peacefully whizzed by their somber embrace.

She sat for hours that night after she surveyed her clueless ninth graders in her contemporary issues class. Most were born around the day of that fateful event, and still, their knowledge base remained void.

Culling through pictures and headlines, articles and diary entries; listening to countless recordings; watching the devastating footage. All served as very jagged pieces to a story Ms. Krueg refused to forget.

Students completed a writing task on the morning of September 11, 2015.

And suddenly, she turned off the lights.

The students, in a quiet curiosity, looked around the classroom.

Ms. Krueg ordered students to rush four floors down to the exit. Her tone was with such seriousness that they followed her directive without question or need for clarification.

Students followed one another, filing through the hallways appropriately, quietly, as Ms. Krueg urged.

Ms. Krueg followed behind, speaking loudly, and rushing students even faster. A sense of panic and urgency was almost contagious as students obliged.

All students reached the first floor, where Ms. Krueg announced that they would be in room 107. They piled in and followed emergency procedures accordingly.

As students huddled into the corner of the room, *nearly out of breath*, Ms. Krueg pushed "play." And that's when students heard the phone calls. The shrillness of the alarms. The helplessness in their tone: These were the people who had many more floors to travel than *just four*. These were the people who were stuck, barricaded on their designated floors by a wall of smoke and fire. Trapped and succumbing to their unfortunate demise.

Students still remained huddled.

Ms. Krueg then handed out newspapers, many frayed on their edges and yellowed over time. They read through the cover article, "America Under Attack." *They were starting to get it.*

Students discussed the events described in their newspaper.

And then Ms. Krueg rolled the footage. Students watched in sullen terror.

But this was history. Ms. Krueg reminded students that this was *their history*. And this was the truth.

Ms. Krueg has felt some safety in moving to the suburbs, but not all that much has changed for her.

Students sat dumbfounded, with so many questions.

They read. They listened. They watched. They made meaning from everything Ms. Krueg had prepared.

It was important for Ms. Krueg to move away from her podium that day. In bringing this moment from history to life, students could not stop talking about that lesson as a part of their personal history.

And that made all the difference.

Reflection/Discussion Questions

1. What exactly was so special about this specific lesson that Ms. Krueg prepared for students on that day?
2. In preparing her lesson plan, what considerations must Ms. Krueg make? What cautionary steps might she take?
3. What are some lessons worthy of "bringing to life" in the same manner that Ms. Krueg did on this day?

"TWO FOR TIMER"

"You will have ten minutes to complete your discussion on literary devices as related to theme in chapter five of *The Great Gatsby*. We've gone over the guidelines for this discussion, including the goals and rubric, and the bullet-pointed reminders are projected up on the board for your reference. You may begin," Ms. Thorne stated, rather stiffly, as the director of student affairs had just made himself comfortable with an open laptop in the back corner of the room.

Ms. Thorne, a first-year teacher, had been waiting for this dreaded moment for nearly six months now. Her own supervisor had completed two observations, but now it was time for an "objective, third party" to make his judgments on Ms. Thorne's teaching practices. And, maybe because she felt it to be Judgment Day, Ms. Thorne could not present herself in the warm, thoughtful way she generally did in front of her students. Though aware of the stiffness of her body language and the dullness of her tone, Ms. Thorne's nerves made her unable to revert to her normal self.

"Five minutes remaining," Ms. Thorne announced, startled by how unrecognizable her own voice sounded.

Students in this honors-level English class rattled off impressive details about the text.

"I think the epizeuxis of 'hot, hot, hot' seems like it is emphasizing the heat of the outdoors, but really it serves to highlight the increasing tensions between Gatsby and Tom Buchannan."

"I'd have to agree. It isn't the first time Fitzgerald used the device to show heightened tensions. Remember in chapter 2 when Myrtle's repetition of Daisy's name led to Tom's physical outburst?"

Ms. Thorne sat back, lovingly, inwardly applauding her students' confidence and sophisticated analysis of the text. "Okay, this observation is actually going pretty well," Ms. Thorne allowed herself to breathe from her desk while the students finished up their discussion.

"That's time."

Ms. Thorne signaled to the students in the outer circle to begin their constructive critique of the inner circle's discussion, a second-nature practice at this point in the school year.

A soft-spoken student at the end of the semicircle began, "I thought David did a great job of linking devices to theme."

The next in line, an extroverted, bright female student stated, in a louder tone than Ms. Thorne had been able to muster all period, "Honestly, their conversation was great, but I guess this isn't really a critique of them, but why don't you have a timer projected so that we can keep our own time? It's kind of hard to keep checking the clock when you want to make sure you're paying attention to the conversation."

Several students nodded in agreement. Mr. Director of Student Affairs tapped feverishly on his keyboard.

"Shit," is what Ms. Thorne was really thinking, but she managed to respond, "Annabelle, that's a great idea. For our next discussion, I'll make sure I use the projected timer."

And just like that, Ms. Thorne felt as if the lesson had crumbled. Her confidence was already being tried, but now it had been conquered. It was something so simple. Of course, the timer should be projected. She had had the guidelines on the overheard, feeling as if that alone would be enough to foster this discussion. But, naturally, students needed to be able to monitor their own time.

A few days later, Ms. Thorne met with Mr. Director for her post-observation. Unlike many of the relatable administrators in the district, this director often exuded a feeling of condescendence, and Ms. Thorne felt unnerved being in his office alone, ready for Judgment Day Part II.

"The students really know the material, Ms. Thorne, so they did a great job."

"Here it comes," Ms. Thorne thought.

"So, as far as the content of the lesson, I think it's clear that students are absorbing the lessons you're teaching and applying that knowledge accurately."

An inward, "Yes!"

"But,"

An inward, "No!"

"As Annabelle pointed out, and I have Annabelle as one of my own students and I know she can be a little bitch (an inward, "Did he really just say that?!"), but a visible timer for an activity like this is really crucial. These are students who want to know how many seconds they have left. They care a lot about being heard."

Ms. Thorne ignored the expletive: "I know. I'll make sure I have the timer projected next time. I'm embarrassed that I forgot it this time."

"And one other thing, Thorne. You know you're on stage when you're a teacher, right? So, that means it doesn't matter if you haven't slept or you're having a bad day, you need to really show up and sell that lesson."

"Uh, yes, of course. I think I just got a little nervous with you in the room, and I wasn't acting like myself."

"Well, like I said, you're an actor when you're up there. The kids shouldn't ever know if something is fazing you."

"Okay. Thank you," Ms. Thorne walked out of the room, sheepishly.

She checked her observation scores the next day.

The overall average score put Ms. Thorne in the "Effective Teacher" category, but as she scrolled through, she noticed: "1d Demonstrating Knowledge of Resources: 2."

And this category was not the only that indicated what Ms. Thorne could only deem "ineptitude" as far as she was concerned.

The burden of the forgotten timer weighed on Ms. Thorne as she read through the rest of the observation. Memories of the meeting would weave in and out of her subconscious while she did so, and she wondered what her face must have looked like when the director of student affairs called a fifteen-year-old a "little bitch."

Reflection/Discussion Questions

1. How can a teacher make sure she has accounted for all available and necessary resources before beginning a lesson?
2. How should Ms. Thorne have reacted to Annabelle during the observation? Was Annabelle's comment appropriate?
3. How should an administrator and a teacher speak to one another during a post-observation? Was Mr. Director's commentary appropriate? Were Ms. Thorne's responses appropriate?

"I DON'T JUDGE THEM BY THEIR SKIN COLOR"

"My mother danced all night and Roberta's was sick," begins Toni Morrison's short story "Recitatif."

Twelfth-grade English teacher Mr. Frederick remembered "Recitatif" as he began planning a unit on Morrison's *The Bluest Eye*. *The Bluest Eye*, he thought, should be taught with emphasis on human tendency to pass judgment based upon skin color. His mind raced while he thought of the intense discussions he would facilitate regarding societal subjugation, stereotypes, racialized beauty standards, and cyclical repression. He anticipated that students would research some of those ideas as they related to the 1940s context of *The Bluest Eye*, Morrison's time of writing in the 1980s and, finally, the relevance of those concepts in the present. Despite the bleak content of the novel, Mr. Frederick felt nothing short of excited to begin the unit, which he was sure was the most relevant of the entire year.

What Mr. Frederick loved about "Recitatif" was Morrison's tactful cleverness in leaving the races of the two orphaned female protagonists undisclosed. Morrison directs readers of the story to infer that one of the young girls is white and one is black, as the duo is referred to as, "salt and pepper." Interspersing stereotypes throughout, Morrison never reveals outright which child is black and which is white. By the end of reading the short story, though, without fail, many readers have, inadvertently, made several judgments.

With intentional minimal direction, Mr. Frederick asked his class to read "Recitatif" as an introductory assignment. Only two of the twenty-eight seniors raised their hands while reading to individually ask Mr. Frederick if Twyla or Roberta was the white character. Mr. Frederick put a finger to his lips, and made both students feel that they were in on a very cunning secret.

Students busily read and annotated the short story, given only the directive of highlighting characteristics of each of the protagonists.

At the end of forty-five minutes of independent reading time, Mr. Frederick directed the class to look up at the projection screen. There were three simple questions displayed: What ethnic background is Twyla? What ethnic background is Roberta? How do you know?

Mr. Frederick asked students to take five minutes to discuss their answers in small groups, and to write down their rationales. Students immediately began discussing, and with great satisfaction, Mr. Frederick immediately noticed the debates.

"No, Twyla is black because her name is Twyla," one student commented.

"But, Roberta has to be black because her mother shows up with a Bible," another responded.

Mr. Frederick would not budge on the issue until the five minutes were up and simply told students to keep discussing and writing down their rationales.

"Okay, so let's settle this once and for all," Mr. Frederick began, "I'm going to do a whip around of groups, and I want you to tell me the answers to the questions listed on the board."

Students, excitedly, pled their cases, and Mr. Frederick was thrilled that they had taken the bait for this assignment. Student after student rattled off one stereotype after the next about why one character was definitely black and why one was definitely white.

"Can anyone find a part of the text that explicitly states which character is white or black?" Mr. Frederick looked out at his pupils.

They feverishly skimmed back through the pages. To no avail; there was no mention of designated race.

Mr. Frederick displayed the next slide. There were more discussion questions: Do we often pass judgments on others simply based upon learned stereotypes? What stereotypes did you make while you were reading?

The bell rang, and Mr. Frederick turned this would-be discussion into a journal activity due the next day.

Students left the room still chatting about the short story, and Mr. Frederick patted himself on the back for his crafty introduction to the unit's most troubling issues.

Journal entries were due electronically by 5 p.m. the next day on a site Mr. Frederick used frequently. Curious to read the responses, Mr. Frederick logged on that same evening to begin checking the homework assignment.

Sipping a post-gym smoothie, Mr. Frederick kicked back on his couch and logged onto the journal site. He read several reactions in which students were really surprised at their own hasty judgments. He read several others in which students felt they only made the judgments because they were directed to and that they did not actually succumb to them. "Political answer," thought Mr. Frederick.

And then Mr. Frederick came upon one response that left him open mouthed. It went something like this:

"Mr. Frederick, I honestly don't get this assignment. I have plenty of friends, and I don't judge them on their skin color. I don't think that if their mom has a certain profession that its because they're black or white. Having us try to point out racial stereotypes makes me really uncomfortable, and I do not want to complete the rest of this assignment."

Mr. Frederick's stomach dropped.

He had the standard first-year-teacher thoughts when anything goes awry, "Wow, did I really mess up this time? Did all of the students find the assignment offensive? Are they going to tell their parents? Am I going to be fired?"

Mr. Frederick tried not to be impulsive but used the reply feature on the website to type a quick message: "Alyssa, the intention of this assignment was to simply get everyone thinking about how and why we stereotype. We will discuss in class tomorrow why this could be a good opening to the unit."

Mr. Frederick shut his computer. That was enough grading for the night.

Reflection/Discussion Questions

1. How should a teacher approach a unit in which controversial issues need to be discussed?
2. Was Mr. Frederick's assignment insensitive? How could he have made his intentions clearer?
3. Should Mr. Frederick report the student's response to an administrator? To a parent? Should he talk to the student individually?

"MULTIPLE-CHOICE"

In life, we get no do-overs.

That's what Ms. Freeman has always learned.

It was the day of the class's unit test. And students were nervous. These were the types of students who were hyperfocused on getting good grades, and Ms. Freeman knew it.

She was known for her difficult tests.

Students walked in to find that the test was already face down on their desks. Ms. Freeman presented a timer, giving students five minutes to review their notes.

Their *notes*—Ms. Freeman didn't believe in study guides.

The timer dinged, and like well-trained golden retrievers, they flipped over their tests and began working.

Of course, there were different versions placed about the room. Students didn't even bother looking over at their neighbor's paper, as some tests were printed on different colored paper, while others had different questions entirely.

Each trudged through Ms. Freeman's tricky multiple-choice questions, set with specific traps, almost to "get" students. Students maneuvered carefully, checking their work over and over again.

The timer continued to be projected at the front of the classroom.

They had 22 minutes and 40 seconds left.

As time wound down, students felt their hands get clammy. Ms. Freeman moved about the room, weaving in and out of the carefully designed, perfectly straight rows. The click of her high heels added another layer of anxiety to the overfocused test takers.

One minute remaining. Students rushed, fervently swiping the eraser remnants from the tops of their desks.

It was a tough assessment. Ms. Freeman and the rest of the class knew it.

Students handed in their work, some shamed by its difficulty, others with pompous confidence. To close, Ms. Freeman repeated the weekend's homework.

The homework was pretty standard for Ms. Freeman's class: *Please read pages 67–90. Complete exercises 1–10 on the last page of your reading.*

Her addition of "please" was Ms. Freeman's attempt at being lighter in tone with her students. At times, her students found this to be comical.

In sitting down that evening to review the pile of tests, Ms. Freeman's red pen would strike through answers, leaving a large "X" over each incorrect response. She would take off points if students did not appropriately show their work.

Ultimately, almost all of the students failed that day.

The testing procedures. The timer. The wasted time in monitoring their work. *All for nothing.*

Ms. Freeman took a step back. She looked over the questions once more. And stopped for a moment.

Sometimes, we blame students for a job awfully done.

And *sometimes*, the results of an assessment reveal the truth of how well we really taught the content in the first place.

Reflection/Discussion Questions

1. In Ms. Freeman's reflection, what could she have changed about this particular assessment? How could she have adjusted her procedures to garner trust?
2. How did Ms. Freeman know that there were issues with this assessment? At what point is it the student's fault in failure to score well, and at what point is it the teacher's?
3. How should Ms. Freeman move forward from this testing day? What steps would you take to rectify the class's situation?

TWO

The Classroom Environment

Aside from the tantalizing coffee concoctions and the irresistible treats that Starbucks boasts, one of the main reasons for their success has been their ability to make the establishment feel like "the third place." Customers come in and are instantly immersed in an environment that reminds them just enough of home to get comfortable and just enough of work to be productive. The playlists are catchy but not distracting, the baristas are pleasant, and the lighting just dim enough to ease your tensions and bright enough to keep you alert. Undoubtedly, countless highly educated professionals discussed, debated, and tested different options until Starbucks finally reached that beloved title of "the third place." While no teacher will have a team of experts choosing comfortable lounge chairs or testing just the right level of dimness, it is important that we consider, thoroughly, the environment of our own classrooms.

Teachers should often think of the third place as inspiration for classroom design. Students need to feel comfortable enough, literally, to voice their opinions, write for extended periods of time, crunch equations, lay out timelines, look at maps, distinguish colors and numbers, and have meaningful peer interactions. Creating a comfortable environment is not an easy task but one for which all teachers should strive, even when resources are limited. This might come in the form of changing the shape of the arrangement of desks in the room, taking into account visibility, or even taking student surveys for the purpose of preference.

Aside from the physical environment, the most important aspects of a classroom environment are the figurative ones. It sounds simple enough: make sure students feel safe in your classroom, make sure they are respectful to you and to one another, make sure they feel ready and able to learn and to succeed.

In an ideal world, all of the above happens like clockwork, but the truth is that establishing a productive, respectful, comfortable classroom environment takes a lot of hard work and reflection. Just as Starbucks, though, has mastered the ability to make consumers eager to return, careful planning and reflection along the way can make a teacher's classroom have that same feeling of comfort and motivation on its students.

"SOMEWHERE IN THE MIDDLE"

She sat there, eyes vacant, as Mr. Philmore reviewed the course syllabus.

He scanned the classroom, identifying and judging who would be those who did too much and those who did too little.

Calculating up and down through the classroom desks, interweaving purposefully, eyeing students in their small pods. The click of his shoes was hard, as students raised their hands to ask the most appropriate of questions.

She continued to sit, while Mr. Philmore continued to plot.

Mr. Philmore's voice echoed and reverberated in that classroom adorned with student work and college admissions acceptance letters. The very reminder of this being a high-caliber class was reemphasized as students looked at the graded student essays surrounding them on the classroom walls.

Her name was Donata, and even from this perspective, the very first day of her eleventh-grade year, she refused to attempt to make a first impression. Donata would roll her eyes every now and then, almost in an attempt to get Mr. Philmore to be offended in some way. Every now and then, Mr. Philmore would dart looks at Donata if she was not fully engaged in the classroom dialogue. She continued to do it on purpose just to get a rise from Mr. Philmore. Mr. Philmore tried his hardest; after all, a good teacher was a patient one.

Mr. Philmore, though, was far from patient, and tried his best to shift his personal drawbacks into his professional strengths. Finding this balance continued to be a struggle, especially in his first year of teaching.

The students turned in their first written pieces, perched upon fresh slices of printer paper—efforts in Times New Roman, size 12 font. Mr. Philmore collected the work in one large mass, having students send up classwork to the front of the classroom. As he neatened the pile, Mr. Philmore would give a glance to those students who did not turn in their homework.

After all, Mr. Philmore had high expectations for students. He refused to accept late work, and used this as some sort of power play in giving credence to his course. He wanted to prepare his students for college and would stop at nothing to give his students the proper experience.

Classroom lectures, coupled with supplemental materials helped to create classroom dialogue that was fruitful and worthwhile, always peppered with a seriousness that served as a reminder that Mr. Philmore taught like a college professor—like his favorite college professors, really. His intimidating stature almost made students feel exhausted, and his firing of questions left students wanting to please Mr. Philmore for the sake of being quick.

Why did the writer use this tone in the first paragraph of this passage?
What is strong about this piece of writing?
Why?
How do we know?
What does this mean?

And the questions would go on. The fastest answers were rewarded the most. Mr. Philmore would high-five, would cackle in glee, and would brag about his future college pupils. They were on their way, and in this fashion, they were on their way because of Mr. Philmore—his high standards were met by his students, even the students who struggled the most. This, essentially, made Mr. Philmore feel like he was doing something right.

And indeed he was.

Donata's work and efforts remained somewhere in the middle—every assignment, in every marking period. As the teacher, he perpetuated this mediocrity, dictating with red pen as his scepter, and the adjusted rubric as his throne. Donata wanted to be a writer, and Mr. Janks perseverated over the fact that Donata had to be better if she wanted to pursue a career in journalism.

Donata would raise her hand every now and then; she would participate in the class's online discussion board (back then, this online platform was a "new wave" of education); she was much better over a computer screen than she was in person. In fact, Donata's hair often fell over her eyes, and Mr. Philmore would remind Donata to sit up straight.

Mr. Philmore's candor is what helped gain him accolades from the onset of his teaching career. His in-your-face-ness got students talking, and if the kids were talking, Mr. Philmore felt that he was still relevant.

Mr. Philmore has learned, as a now-educational leader, that he was doing it all wrong, and while Donata was lost in the middle, she was really just left behind like those who embraced being average.

Mr. Philmore looks around now and sees what all other assistant principals and principals see—classrooms filled with faces that are pressured, *by everything*. And those at the middle, they still remain—they're okay with their place in the pedagogical pecking order.

Mr. Philmore remembers that she tried. She would write. She spent that time. And he was so focused, as the resident newbie, that he had something to prove. Mr. Philmore looked young. He felt young. He was young. His hair spiked in a way that still kept him relevant. And he was teaching high school. He was touted as a strong teacher, but that's because those students who got lost in the mix of things often did not have a voice.

The teacher doesn't know whatever happened to Donata, but he does know that, in retrospect, *he was wrong*. It is not because he did not care, but it is because he really did not understand.

As a first-year teacher, Mr. Philmore, at times, made it more about his own professional self, rather than the progress of his students. There were other students, much like Donata, whose names may have been forgotten. Their silence is what Mr. Philmore, in looking at his former self, ignored.

Donata sat in the middle, with no phone calls from home; she earned a B, but could have worked to an A, with some more guidance.

While the middle has always been safe, Mr. Philmore is starting to learn *that the middle is often more dangerous than it ever had been before.*

Reflection/Discussion Questions

1. What about Mr. Philmore's former self should have been adjusted midyear in working with students like Donata? What strategies could have been in place to move these types of students forward?
2. How did Mr. Philmore confuse his own perception of himself as a teacher? How do we mend that difference between perception and reality in reflection of our professional selves?
3. Why exactly do you think Mr. Philmore started his career in this manner? What worked about his methodologies?

"I HAVE NO MOUTH AND I MUST SCREAM"

I have no mouth. And I must scream.

Like a mantra, Ms. Johnson found herself reciting Ellison's closing lines under her breath on the afternoon of THS's Day of Silence—an annual occurrence that serves to remind members of the school community of those who have been harassed, marginalized, forced into submission for their sexuality.

That morning, Ms. Johnson picked up her rainbow-colored "Vocal Supporter" sticker and placed it, proudly, on the arm of her blazer. She happily set up computers and a projected discussion board for silent students—a means to elucidate their thoughts during a scheduled Socratic circle.

Students, silent and vocal, filed into the classroom, took their seats and watched docilely while the Friday video announcements streamed. The segment for Day of Silence left this particularly mature, sympathetic group of students staring thoughtfully at the screen, and Ms. Johnson felt a tinge of gratification. Times are changing, she thought.

The Socratic discussion commenced. The clock ticked onward. The bell rang. Students scrambled to gather pencil cases, binders, and brown paper bags. Ms. Johnson stood near the doorway while the ambling mass moved to period 2. As the last student exited, Ms. Johnson turned to find that it was not the last student.

"Ryan, is everything okay?" Ms. Johnson questioned as Ryan, an openly transgender student, fumbled with his hands, gesturing frantically in sign language—an ability he and Ms. Johnson shared.

"Ryan, you can speak in here if something is wrong and continue the day of silence when you leave. I need to know what's going on."

Ryan, stubborn in his pursuit to remain vigilant to this cause, supplemented his sign language with a written note.

When Ms. Johnson first encountered Harlan Ellison's post-apocalyptic science fiction story, it was in a room full of eager graduate students. No one seemed quite as perturbed as she had been when the story reached its conclusion.

In the narrative, machines become intelligent beings and carry out a mass genocide that kills everyone but one woman and four men. In an effort to torture the remaining humans, the machines keep the humans cooped up in an underground complex. The machines starve the humans to near death but then feed them grotesque food periodically to keep them alive. The humans venture one day to find food, and upon finding stores of victuals, realize they are unable to open any of them. Ted, one of the remaining humans, knows that in order to be truly free, they will have to die. He begins killing the humans one by one until only he remains. When the machines realize his intent, they make it impossible for him to take his own life by turning Ted into an amorphous being who lacks the ability to do, well, anything—he cannot speak, he lacks all autonomy, and he must dwell in this complex for eternity at the will of the machines. The story ends when Ted makes the bleak realization: "I have no mouth. And I must scream."

Ms. Johnson read Ryan's note with the same choked feeling she had had when that story concluded. Ryan's scribbled handwriting invited Ms. Johnson into the perpetual harassment that he had faced from a classmate in the very class that, just a few moments earlier, made Ms. Johnson beam with pride. Ryan's note explained that Sarah regularly made threats against him and some of his friends, who had also openly identified against heteronormativity. On this particular day, Ryan's frustrations came to a head, for Sarah roamed the halls, boasting a rainbow "Vocal Supporter" sticker.

"I just can't bear to see it," the note confessed.

"Ryan, I need to go to guidance to tell them about everything you've been going through."

"Okay," Ryan conceded with a shoulder shrug.

Ryan proceeded to his next class, and Ms. Johnson, shaken, sat in the department office for a moment, gathering herself before going to guidance.

"I have no mouth. And I must scream," Ms. Johnson mouthed to herself, feeling the tangibility of the concept that once shook her.

Ms. Johnson sorted her stack of papers, threw her I.D. in her bag, and jumped a bit when there was a steady knock at the department office door.

"Ryan, what are you doing here? Aren't you supposed to be in class? I was just going to the guidance office."

"Ms. Johnson, you can't go! You can't go! Please don't go!"

An eruption of tears accompanied Ryan's plea. Ms. Johnson stood in awe, dumbfounded by the verbal command—a sacred vow of silence broken in desperation.

"If you go to guidance, she will know it was me and she will come after me and you don't understand what she has done to me and my friends. You don't understand," Ryan's chest heaved up and down as he breathlessly begged with the will of someone fighting for his life.

"Okay, okay, Ryan, I won't go," Ms. Johnson assured.

Reverting to some latent comforting skills, Ms. Johnson calmed Ryan down enough for him to take full breaths.

Having regained composure, Ryan, relieved but broken, once again continued to class.

Ms. Johnson, hand on hip, breathed out a sigh in the solitude of the department office. She pondered her responsibility: "Legally, I must speak," she thought to herself. "Morally, I must speak. Morally, though, I must not."

Ms. Johnson, unsure if it was the image of a broken child's languid gait or the memory of the amorphous, silenced, helpless Ted, knew what she must do.

She stood with her hand on the door of an office titled "Ms. Murtori, Guidance Counselor," repeating her mantra as she twisted the knob.

Reflection/Discussion Questions

1. How should Ms. Johnson have handled Ryan's initial confession at the close of the class period?
2. Should Ms. Johnson have honored Ryan's request not to go to the guidance department? What other actions could she have taken?
3. How can Ms. Johnson ensure her classroom is a safe place, in which bullying does not occur behind the scenes?

"6:00 P.M."

The first week of school. Every night at 6:00 p.m. Ms. Rais would finish her dinner and plan on making her phone calls.

She had just met her fourth graders for the first time this week. As a class, Ms. Rais already had the opportunity to get to know her students. At this point, even after just a few days, Ms. Rais could discern the twenty-two different personalities and learning styles that made each student truly unique.

She was excited to get started. These calls always made Ms. Rais a little anxious, but she knew that they were important.

The phone would ring. Usually, Ms. Rais prayed that the voice mail would answer so that she could give her pitch to a machine, rather than the parent themselves.

Of course, though, the parent almost always answered:

"Hello, is this Mr. Grant? My name is Ms. Rais and I am Annie's fourth-grade teacher. I wanted to call to introduce myself. Annie is off to a great start this school year. Already, she has taken a liking to the reading centers in our classroom!"

"Well, thank you for calling," Mr. Grant quickly replied.

Ms. Rais gushed, "Not a problem at all. Reach out if you need me for anything!"

Ms. Rais was purposefully enthusiastic—and truly, it was infectious.

The school continued much like it did the year before. There were the ups and downs. The struggles still existed. Parents sometimes questioned Ms. Rais.

But they never forgot the first phone call of the school year—at 6:00 p.m.

Reflection/Discussion Questions

1. Ms. Rais's beginning-of-the-year routine seemed to have an impact on families. What might be some issues that Ms. Rais would face along the way?
2. What are some similar ways that Ms. Rais could "check in" with families? At what point of the year might this be beneficial?
3. In making such phone calls, what specific information should Ms. Rais prepare? How would you change this practice to make it your own?

"STEPHEN"

Mr. Jay's pallid complexion made Ms. Sanchez pause immediately as she read out her roster to one of her more experienced colleagues.

"Okay, in my sixth-grade history class, I have Robert Annelle, Nicole DeMarco, Samantha Dune, Stephen Fracas—"

Mr. Jay put his hand up in a gesture for Ms. Sanchez to stop rattling off names.

"Oh, no," Mr. Jay looked mildly entertained but mostly full of pity for Ms. Sanchez, who would be just beginning her first year at Riley Middle School.

"Stephen Fracas. Let me give you a little background on Stephen Fracas. In fourth grade, *fourth grade*, police did a locker search after hearing some rumors. The kid had an ounce of marijuana at the elementary school. Worse than that, he was on house arrest at age ten. I think this might be his second go-around in sixth grade. He spent a lot of time out last year, rumors of rehab or juvie or one of those."

"You can't be serious." Ms. Sanchez gave Mr. Jay a head-tilted, playful look of inquiry.

Mr. Jay stifled a chuckle, "I'm very serious. Check his notes on the system."

So, Ms. Sanchez did just that. She could see that it was, indeed, Stephen's second time in sixth grade and that there were parental warnings regarding who could and could not pick up the child from school—no mention of rehabilitation or any correctional facilities. "Maybe, Mr. Jay is playing a prank on me," Ms. Sanchez thought. "Perhaps, I'm going through a bit of new-girl hazing."

She decided to keep an open mind when meeting Stephen and hoped her calm demeanor would be enough to help him learn and grow in her classroom.

Stephen showed up on the first day of school dressed in loose-fitting jeans, a polo button-down and a backwards cap.

"Hey! Hat, off!" Ms. Sanchez heard the school disciplinarian yell to Stephen before he stepped into Ms. Sanchez's period 5 history class.

Stephen smacked his lips, begrudgingly removed the cap, and muttered something under his breath.

"Okay, here we go," thought Ms. Sanchez.

Ms. Sanchez greeted everyone, introduced the course, discussed how excited she was to be starting at Riley Middle School. She kept an eye on Stephen, but treated him no differently from everyone else. Aside from the hat incident at the start of class, she thought his behavior was fine.

She caught up with Mr. Jay after class. "He was fine," Ms. Sanchez gloated a bit.

Mr. Jay shrugged his shoulders, "You'll see."

And Ms. Sanchez did see. Stephen became comfortable quite quickly in Ms. Sanchez's class. Pretty soon, he felt it his liberty to blurt out comments at any moment, to touch the students around him, to walk around the room.

Ms. Sanchez asked Stephen to stay after class one afternoon.

"Stephen, if there is ever a time when you're feeling really active, you can sign out and go for a walk. And I'd appreciate if you could raise your hand when you have an answer. The calling out can be distracting for everyone, you know?"

Stephen, sarcastically, replied, "You got it, Ms. Sanchez," and walked away with not a care in the world.

Nothing changed. Stephen had been placed next to nearly every student in class. His longest placement was next to a particularly quiet, well-behaved student, Molly.

One day after class, Molly appeared next to the teacher's desk. "Ms. Sanchez, do you think we could change seats soon? Stephen keeps making snake sounds and touching my feet under the desk when you're not looking and it kind of scares me."

Ms. Sanchez ashamed at this confession, said, "Oh, Molly, I'm sorry. Yes, we'll change seats tomorrow. Thank you for working so well with everyone in class."

Ms. Sanchez completed another seat change, but was very aware that her control over this particular student, and as a result, of the class, was dwindling. Stephen continued to call out. At first, his classmates did their best not to react. However, Stephen upped his crudeness as the days ticked on.

Part of the sixth-grade history curriculum was to cover the Jewish migration in the Mediterranean, and Stephen blurted out, "Were the Jews on their ways to get burned alive?" He laughed a full-bodied laugh after he finished his question.

Ms. Sanchez sent him to the disciplinarian. He strutted out of the room; some of the more self-conscious students laughed, while most of the others looked on in amusement but disgust.

Ms. Sanchez would send Stephen out of the room countless times that year. His after-school and Saturday detentions totaled more than he could feasibly complete in one school year; he did not care.

Ms. Sanchez, eventually, became frustrated. She had rearranged the room, spoken to Stephen personally, gone to guidance, attempted to call home (no answer), attempted to e-mail home (no answer), and finally, just ran her class as well as she could while ignoring Stephen's outbursts.

Ms. Sanchez had tried being kind and understanding, pulling Stephen from his support class to chat, like adults over coffee (in a public space), about his behavior. She had tried being stern and unyielding; nothing changed Stephen's behavior, and she began to feel personally victimized by a twelve-year-old.

During a pop-in observation, the assistant principal visited Ms. Sanchez's class. While she was on one end of the room and Stephen on the other, he blurted out, "Look who it is, the Lizard Bitch."

Those who heard him snickered. Ms. Andy had not, for which Ms. Sanchez was very thankful. This was not Stephen's first time, unapologetically insulting a faculty member.

On another occasion, a member of the math department escorted Stephen back to class after he had been roaming the library aimlessly during class time. The math teacher interrupted Ms. Sanchez's class to announce, "I found this," he gestured disgustedly toward Stephen while pulling a bit on Stephen's shirt collar, "roaming around the library. Did you check the time he signed out?"

"Let me go, you Santa Claus looking fuck," Stephen shouted in Mr. Augusta's bearded face.

Mr. Augusta stormed out of Ms. Sanchez's room.

Ms. Sanchez spoke to Stephen, to the class about respect, and later in the day wrote up the incident. She also went to visit Mr. Augusta to apologize for Stephen's disrespect the next day; she noticed he had shaved his beard.

Ms. Sanchez spent more of her time disciplining Stephen than she did teaching the class. While no other student rivaled Stephen's level of disrespect, it did make students feel like they, themselves, could push the limits. Hand raising seemed to have become optional, unrelated comments suddenly appropriate. Just one student had compromised the academic integrity of Ms. Sanchez's course.

When Stephen was absent, Ms. Sanchez was thankful. When he was quiet, she could breathe easier. But most days were a battle. Ms. Sanchez endured the remainder of the year. Every time the bell rang to release that particular period, she was shamelessly relieved. Colleagues offered Ms. Sanchez advice, but she stopped taking it at a certain point.

"Get through this year, and you will not have to teach him again," Ms. Sanchez would think.

Eventually, the year came to a close. When Stephen's final grade affirmed he had failed the course, neither his guidance counselor, nor his parents reached out to Ms. Sanchez.

As Stephen exited Ms. Sanchez's class for the final time, Mr. Disciplinarian, right on cue, reprimanded, "Hat!"

Reflection/Discussion Questions

1. Should Ms. Sanchez have asked a colleague about students before the start of the school year?
2. Were Ms. Sanchez's ways of "handling" Stephen appropriate? What other ways could Ms. Sanchez have tried to get through to Stephen?
3. Without parental support, how can a teacher best challenge and foster a child's education? What else could Ms. Sanchez or the school district have done to support Stephen?

"A CHANGE IN PLANS"

Mrs. Leyton loved her to-do lists.

A view into her home would portray many straight lines and 90-degree angles. Her furniture was something out of a Crate and Barrel catalog—and all of her neighbors knew it. The soft colors. The manicured lawn. Her family resembled a cluster of J. Crew models.

What was so interesting was that Mrs. Leyton's classroom looked much the same way. Her bulletin boards were pristine. High-quality glossy paper served as its surface, and the paper cutouts of the alphabet were so perfectly scissor cut that one would swear that they were custom made just for her. Her craftsmanship seemed to be unparalleled.

These weren't the school materials from the supply closet, and everyone knew it.

Of course, when an administrator entered Mrs. Leyton's room, they immediately responded to the carefully laid bins of school supplies, the laminated classroom schedule presented so perfectly over the classroom pencil sharpener, and the way that her desk was adjusted *just so*. They were always impressed. And rightfully so.

The next forty minutes would be spent on introducing students, or rather, students introducing each other to ecosystems.

Around the room four tables were set up, each with accompanying groups of chairs. At these stations, clear directions were typed up and presented to students. Although in fifth grade, Mrs. Leyton worked to make her students as independent as possible. She called them her mini-adults and in her classroom, she called the learning process "organized chaos."

"The only great way to teach is to have the students teach themselves," Mrs. Leyton often pontificated.

An intellectual hum could be heard if you passed Mrs. Leyton's classroom. And today was no different.

You could hear students discussing coral reefs, watching videos about grassland ecosystems, and debating the differences between estuaries and salt marshes. Each of Mrs. Leyton's twenty-two stars shined brightly that day.

With her hand up, Kayla excitedly asked, "Mrs. Leyton! Is this like the place I went to on vacation last summer in Cozumel?"

Mrs. Leyton responded, "Kayla. Let's focus on our work. Let's answer the questions."

Kayla continued with her group, fervently putting her pencil onto paper—working hard to impress Mrs. Leyton, as was the intent of all the students in this classroom.

The clicking of keyboards added a sort of symphony to the already academic buzz. Some students worked on laptop computers, listening to their video clips before them—multimedia that was already preloaded by Mrs. Leyton before the students even arrived in class.

As students viewed each video and read each relevant article, they navigated from station to station, being guided by the classroom checklist provided by Mrs. Leyton. As each student completed their necessary tasks, they pressed their pencils onto the checklist to make each gratifying mark in each designated, purposeful square. It became quickly obvious that Mrs. Leyton's need for organization was contagious.

Students rarely asked questions and moved swiftly, being reminded by a soft chime from a classroom timer that the one task should be completed and the next should be started. Like well-mannered, conditioned laboratory mice. (Not rats, though, because these students were way too cute.)

Kayla politely raised her hand, awaiting Mrs. Leyton's approval, "Mrs. Leyton! I think I saw a coral reef in Cozumel once!"

Mrs. Leyton followed with, "Okay, Kayla. Now let's get completed with our task."

Mrs. Leyton circulated the classroom mindfully. At times, she would fiddle with her charcoal gray pencil skirt, adjusting it so that its base hit precisely above her knee.

Students continued their usual buzz and Mrs. Leyton watched intently. Every now and then, a student needed a pencil-sharpener break. The grinding of the pencil sharpener contributed to the academic symphony of Mrs. Leyton's classroom.

Kayla raised her hand again.

Mrs. Leyton stopped everything. She did so by raising her hand. All students followed Mrs. Leyton's lead, became silent, and mimicked her hand in the air.

Great teaching is sometimes veering away from the most carefully laid plans.

Reflection/Discussion Questions

1. Of Mrs. Leyton's procedures in class, which do you think work best for the students in this particular class?
2. What might be a reason to not halt or completely adjust your lesson plan? Conversely, at what point might you have to make such significant alterations to your original plan?
3. Think of Kayla. How do the practices in this specific classroom impact students like her? How do you manage the excited ones most appropriately?

"CHARACTER DEGRADATION"

It was through vaguely cracked eyelids that Ms. Newman discovered that she had become victim who-knows-how-many of a form of unforeseeable character degradation.

Betraying every bit of her knowledge of the classics, Ms. Newman had always expected that her adversaries would come in troves, announced, unmistakable, weapon wielding, chest pounding, blood of victims strewn proudly on their being. At the very least, she trusted her self-proclaimed sixth-sense-like intuition and her newly thickened inner-city student-teaching-experienced skin to face her opponents with confidence, assurance, and a cool air of indifference. And so, like Poseidon's doomed heir, Polyphemus, Ms. Newman was left in utter astonishment when the singed spike of disloyalty thrust itself, unapologetically, into her third eye.

Samantha came to class early every afternoon. She was the quintessential go-to student. If an unfocused student needed focusing, he was seated with Samantha. If a controversial issue arose, Samantha acted as the voice of wisdom, gently quelling disputes with a grace that left Ms. Newman feeling shamefully envious. When a proposed question left her peers apathetically blinking, Samantha's hand would jut in the air, palpably breaking the often impenetrable reticence of a sleepy adolescent room. As a first-year teacher, Ms. Newman was sometimes hesitant to bring in course materials that she feared were too advanced, too risqué, too not-teenager-friendly, but Samantha's presence meant that Ms. Newman could introduce college-level material, that someone in the room would be able to comprehend, to digest, to relay information to the rest of the students.

It would be simply untrue if Ms. Newman denied that Samantha had quickly become her favorite student, though she tried her very best to remain as neutral as humanly possible.

So, on a weekday morning, when the first rays of morning light penetrated Ms. Newman's childhood bedroom and a too-often-snoozed alarm blared, Samantha was the furthest person from Ms. Newman's mind. Ms. Newman tapped, almost blindly, at her cell phone until she realized there was an influx of messages from a group chat that she used to keep in touch with high school friends.

"Strange," she thought, "I just checked my phone before bed a few hours ago."

The delirium of a.m. drowsiness quickly transformed itself into heart-pounding distress. In her group chat was a screenshot of a tweet.

Ms. Newman, months prior, had purged all traces of social media from her life. No more Facebook or Instagram or Snapchat or even Pinterest. Life in the real world meant a clean slate in the realm of the Internet. Ms. Newman vowed to be untraceable in a society that felt to her, many times, uncomfortably transparent. A couple of months into the school year, though, Ms. Newman went to a workshop in which the main speaker claimed that she used Twitter as her platform to post about all of her upcoming events, her latest technological finds, and so on. Ms. Newman, breaking her vow of social media purity, innocently enough, opened a Twitter account. Using her childhood screen name as her handle, Ms. Newman or @QTNewGirl, engulfed herself in the world of celebrity news, literary updates, and friendly banter.

Staring at the glow of her cell phone, Ms. Newman instantly regretted her broken vow. Hands shaking, Ms. Newman sat up in her full-sized bed and read the first (of many) student criticisms that she would face as a first-year teacher.

"Ms. Newman assigns the dumbest sh**. What a dumb b**** #QTNewGirl #Growup"

The tweet had been posted by @SammyGirl, and the accompanying profile picture belonged to the face of none other than her beloved, model student, Samantha. Now, Ms. Newman had experienced romantic heartbreak, familial upsets, cataclysmic friendship rifts, but in less than 140 characters, the tweet produced in her an ache that no amount of soothing, at the time, could soften. The multiple layers of the tweet accounted for some of the hurt feelings. Samantha had attacked both the teacher and the teaching—a profession for which Ms. Newman spent tireless hours prepping, sometimes prepping with Samantha in mind. The other layer was that a click on the QTNewGirl hashtag actually brought users to Ms. Newman's personal Twitter account—a feature that Ms. Newman was not sure if Samantha knew about or not. This very feature is what led Ms. Newman to wake up to a screenshot of the tweet. One of Ms. Newman's friends had been on Ms. Newman's account, and the hashtag that Samantha posted using a public account was visible for Ms. Newman's "followers."

So, Ms. Newman sat upright, surrounded by the hot pink walls of her childhood, feeling as small as the day her father let her pick out the color at Lowe's ten years prior.

Ms. Newman pondered many questions: "Why does Samantha work so diligently if she hates the class? If she hates me? Did she know I'd be able to see the tweet? Does she care? Do the other students hate me? Do they, too, think the work I assign is useless?"

Unsure of all of the above, Ms. Newman felt the first logical move was to delete the Twitter account, remove any link between her and the tweet that would etch itself into her memory. Her next move was uncertain.

Despite the pre-sunrise events, Ms. Newman instinctively turned the nozzle in the shower, stepped in, and mentally went through her options. She could report the tweet to administration, but would that get her anywhere? Would she, somehow, be accountable for the student's tweet?

Could she get in trouble for having a Twitter account? Afraid and embarrassed, Ms. Newman decided to do nothing at all.

That day at school, Samantha showed up early, looked Ms. Newman in the eyes, smiled and took her seat at the front of the room. Ms. Newman taught that class period in the same way many experience funerals: out of body, detached. She went through the motions until the bell rang, freeing her from the confines of her self-created prison.

Instead of speaking up about the incident to a coworker, to an administrator, to Samantha, Ms. Newman let the pages of the calendar tear away until she no longer had to face Samantha. Outwardly, nothing changed. Samantha remained the model student and Ms. Newman the consummate professional.

Just as she had vowed to purge herself of all social media, Ms. Newman also vowed to take the incident to the grave—finally, a vow Ms. Newman actually would keep.

Reflection/Discussion Questions

1. Should Ms. Newman have reported the Twitter incident to an administrator?
2. Should Ms. Newman have confronted the student? What are ways to foster growth in exceptional students without it leading to favoritism?
3. How do you think it impacts the classroom environment when one student is relied upon so heavily? When it comes to social media, what actions should a teacher take to ensure privacy and safety?

"QUICKSAND"

Every single morning, Mr. Grohs would check his student roster against the school absentee report. He prayed to see his name.

He never did.

A.J. was a nice boy, and nice to a point where, as a teacher, you could not quite discipline him in an appropriate way.

In fact, A.J. was worse than the student who shouted out in the middle of class or the student who was blatantly rude. But no, A.J. pushed Mr. Grohs to the brink and then self-corrected just in time for Mr. Grohs to make a move—to write him up, to keep him after class, *anything*.

And students were too old to start tattling on each other.

When Mr. Grohs would work on the blackboard, he could feel A.J. whispering, making a face, or tossing a pen cap that would land softly enough not to make a sound. As Mr. Grohs turned around, A.J. sat in silence. A small grin grew slightly on the faces of those students surrounding A.J., but A.J., he remained stoic.

This frustrated Mr. Grohs the most.

He somehow felt that he was losing a battle against a much younger battalion.

Mr. Grohs handed out the tests. Students repositioned their desks so that they formed rows that faced the front of the classroom. Mr. Grohs circulated in the classroom, looking down every now and then at A.J.'s desk for an expected cheat sheet.

The only thing on the desk was A.J.'s test. This time, he wrote out his entire name in red ink: *Anthony Joseph*.

Mr. Grohs continued to trust his gut, however.

To his friends, Mr. Grohs would liken the experience to drowning in quicksand. He felt stuck. He felt helpless. His parents reminded Mr. Grohs that he was being dramatic. His mother was a retired teacher and had been through it all.

She suggested that he just grin and bear it.

And he tried. He really did try.

A.J. would raise his hand, participate in class, and contribute snarky comments. At times, his commentary left Mr. Grohs confused and left the rest of the class in some sort of muffled snickering. Mr. Grohs was obviously the one left out of the joke.

Any one of A.J.'s perceived niceties sparked Mr. Grohs's skepticism. In asking A.J.'s other teachers about his behavior throughout the rest of the school day, all other subject-area teachers gushed over A.J.

"He's a great student. Really adds a lot to class," Mr. V shared.

"What a wonderful presence. Wish all students were like A.J.," Mrs. Jankowski enthusiastically added.

"I love that kid! Straight-A kind of student," Mrs. Silox reiterated.

Mr. Grohs tried to give A.J. the benefit of the doubt, but a feeling nagged him.

Mr. Grohs called home. A.J.'s mother answered.

"Hello?" she curiously inquired.

Mr. Grohs provided A.J.'s mother with a proper greeting and called to "check in."

"I'm so glad you did," Mrs. Filt followed.

"A.J. has been going through a great deal of 'stuff' lately. With my chemo, and his father's overtime, A.J. hasn't been the same," Mrs. Filt revealed.

The phone conversation only lasted a few minutes after that.

Mr. Grohs found the time to talk to A.J., and although Mr. Grohs still had the sneaking suspicion that A.J. was up to *something* every time he turned his head, he now had a frame of reference.

This didn't make everything okay as Mr. Grohs was determined to catch A.J. *eventually*.

Reflection/Discussion Questions

1. Throughout your reading of this anecdote, what did you find to be most wrong in Mr. Grohs's response to A.J. in the classroom?
2. What realities does this view inside Mr. Grohs's classroom reveal about the teaching experience? How might you have adjusted accordingly?
3. Who is A.J. really? How does our perception of students shape the way in which we interact with them in our daily work?

"MYTH BUSTERS"

Ms. Chopra wanted to culminate her unit on myths by having students create their very own. She gave students specific guidelines to follow, went over her expectations, discussed rubrics, and let the creativity flow.

She looked forward to hearing each of the ninth graders present their tales. They had read and analyzed so many classic myths that Ms. Chopra was sure her group of students would digest some techniques from the classics while infusing their own originality into their work. When the day came for presentations, Ms. Chopra was more excited than the students.

The bolder students volunteered to read their myths first. One student supplemented her reading by turning the room into a pseudo-campfire setting. She turned down the lights, projected an active flame, and kept a flashlight under her face while she read her bone-chilling tale. Ms. Chopra applauded.

Student after student read their myths, each varying in skill, Ms. Chopra appreciating them all.

When Dustin's turn came to read his myth, Ms. Chopra sensed his hesitation. He was definitely never the first student to volunteer so Ms. Chopra assumed he was just experiencing some presentation jitters.

Regardless, he took his position at the front of the room. Mimicking the style of the campfire presenter, he turned down the lights and used a flashlight to illuminate his face.

Dustin began, "There was once an English teacher who assigned very much work." He made eye contact with Ms. Chopra and continued, "And every day, Justin had to go home and type away on his computer to write essays and stories and journal entries."

Ms. Chopra wondered where this was going and thought maybe Dustin was just going to make a mockery of the assignment.

Dustin continued to share a "myth" about an English teacher, who was eerily similar to Ms. Chopra.

He concluded the myth: "And then one day, the English teacher did not show up to school. They found her fingers under Justin's bed, clutching a pencil."

Dustin flicked off the flashlight and took his seat. Students looked at one another and halfheartedly produced a round of snaps, as they had done for the rest of their peers.

When class ended, Ms. Chopra went straight to the guidance office.

She found Mrs. Sanders, Dustin's counselor, and told her the series of events. Ms. Chopra did not know Mrs. Sanders very well because Ms. Chopra had just started teaching in the district that year. She thought, though, that the incident from class that day should be shared with someone else. Ms. Chopra confided in Mrs. Sanders.

"Yeah, so it's probably nothing, but I just wanted to make you aware that Dustin shared a sort of bizarre story with my class. He talked about an 'English teacher' and his dislike for the English teacher and ended the story with the English teacher's fingers being found under his bed. It just struck me as kind of, I don't know, noteworthy," Ms. Chopra stood with her hands clasped in front of her.

Mrs. Sanders looked nothing short of irritated for having her private office time interrupted, and when she slipped her glasses down her nose to assess Ms. Chopra, Ms. Chopra felt instantly vulnerable.

Mrs. Sanders looked Ms. Chopra up and down. Ms. Chopra was wearing one of her favorite outfits she had bought for student teaching, a knee-length designer bright-blue tweed skirt and a tucked-in button-down. She had also worn a matching statement necklace and new flats. Ms. Chopra tucked a piece of hair behind her ear, nervously awaiting Mrs. Sander's expert opinion on the day's events.

"Did you ever think Dustin might just have a crush on you?" Mrs. Sanders asked Ms. Chopra with palpable condescension.

"Er, not really," Ms. Chopra fidgeted, slipping one of her flats on and off her left foot, "I've never really had any significant interactions with him, and his myth definitely didn't make me feel like he thinks of me fondly."

"I'll call Dustin into my office to talk about it," Mrs. Sanders said in a tone that made Ms. Chopra sure their conversation was over.

Ms. Chopra left Mrs. Sanders's office, surprised and shaken. She decided she would talk to Dustin herself the next day.

After the next day's class ended, Ms. Chopra pulled Dustin aside, "Hey, Dustin, I just have a question for you because I'm starting to put in grades for the myths. Was there a reason you went with that kind of plot for your story?"

Dustin looked surprised, "Hm, I don't know I guess I was up late working on the assignment for your class and I thought, 'Imagine if you could just get rid of an assignment.' It was late and the story kind of spiraled into something weird."

"Okay, did you feel like you were angry about the assignment or anything?" Ms. Chopra prodded.

"Ehh, not really. I was just tired and wanted to keep playing World of Warcraft. It didn't take me that long, to be honest."

"Okay, thanks." Ms. Chopra let Dustin leave.

His explanation seemed innocent enough, and Dustin was not aggressive at all when Ms. Chopra confronted him. She decided she would let the events go and wait to hear back from Mrs. Sanders.

Dustin never wrote another red-flag-raising story, but Ms. Chopra never heard back from Mrs. Sanders either.

Reflection/Discussion Questions

1. How should Ms. Chopra have reacted to Dustin's myth?
2. Did she make the right decision by going to guidance? Did the guidance counselor offer appropriate support?
3. Was Ms. Chopra correct to confront Dustin directly? What could have happened?

"SOMETHING DIFFERENT"

Katie fidgeted a lot on this day—more than usual.

Ms. Harrington knew how to handle Katie, but on days like these, Ms. Harrington had to make more adjustments than normal. Quite simply, none of her education courses adequately prepared Ms. Harrington to attend to the needs of Katie.

In working through a lesson about Native American tribes, Katie would tap her desk almost uncontrollably. With each slight tick, Ms. Harrington would address Katie's behavior.

"Let's put these coins away, Katie. Making noises can be distracting to other students," Ms. Harrington cautioned.

Still, the other students, even as young as they were, knew that Katie was different. They gawked at her like she was a freak.

So unassuming, Katie would play with her colored pencils instead of the K-W-L chart Ms. Harrington directed students to fill out. Katie hated worksheets, even as a second grader. She liked activities that were actually active.

Teachers who passed Ms. Harrington's classroom often gave a rolled eye or a glance in Katie's direction. It was hard to not notice Katie as she had obvious trouble with sitting still and remaining quiet, as all second graders are taught to do.

Katie seemed to be the exception.

Ms. Harrington began to lose her patience with Katie midyear. At one point, Ms. Harrington started blaming her own lax regulation of the classroom procedures as the rationale for Katie's outbursts.

Confiding in colleagues, Ms. Harrington did not quite trust her own intuition in addressing the needs of Katie. Searching for answers to her questions, Ms. Harrington was only left with more inquiry.

Ms. Harrington checked Katie's record.

How could she have gone through pre-kindergarten, kindergarten, and first grade without an issue at all?

Katie's mother, when Ms. Harrington would call, quickly darted to a rehearsed, immediate response: "She will not be classified. She isn't one of *those* kids."

Ms. Harrington continued in her attempts at being patient with Katie.

As the school year continued, Katie became more and more inattentive. Ms. Harrington attempted to come up with a reward system, providing Katie with every opportunity to be better in class behaviorally.

The largest struggle was that Katie was a smart little girl. She just refused to sit still. And Katie's mother did not want to hear any of it.

Ms. Harrington had several reasons for Katie's possible outbursts but did not feel nearly qualified to make absolute sense of everything that was going on. All Ms. Harrington knew was that there was something different about Katie.

After tireless attempts at trying to figure Katie out, and even though she felt as if she was turning on Katie's mother, Ms. Harrington decided to turn to the experts.

The experts wanted to evaluate Katie.

Katie's mother refused.

Incidentally, Katie was pulled from school the next week and transferred to a private school nearby.

At first, Ms. Harrington felt terrible, almost guilty.

Until she was reminded, "You did the right thing."

Reflection/Discussion Questions

1. What specific interventions would you have in place in class to help Katie?
2. In observing Katie's behavior, what might be some more possible suggestions you would give to Ms. Harrington in working with Katie through her classroom behavior?
3. After Katie was transferred from this school, Ms. Harrington was told that she "did the right thing." What exactly was Ms. Harrington "right" about?

THREE
Instruction

How to be an Effective Teacher. Teach Like a Champion. The Book Whisperer.

As undergraduates, aspiring educators are bombarded by educational instruction books and texts on pedagogy. Highlighted, underlined, and annotated to smithereens, these wide-eyed future teachers left college feeling as though they had devoured all that they needed in order to deliver instruction really well.

What many of those titles omitted, though, was what happens when you have planned for certain outcomes or have thought you came up with an engaging activity, and it falls flat. Or, you created an assessment, and half of the class showed their understanding and half did not. When it comes to instruction, it is really important to put into effect the lessons from the professionals, but it is equally important to be flexible; one professional's approach to education might just not work for you. For example, in Harry Wong's *First Days of School,* he often stresses the use of repetition to solidify a routine for a student. Well, what happens if that student, brazenly, refuses to complete the act of repetition? Or, in *Teach Like a Champion,* Doug Lemov suggests the technique of discussing incorrect solutions to a problem before revealing the correct response. What if this leaves students baffled and confused?

While formal advice from the experts should certainly play a role in your classroom, keep in mind that flexibility is a really integral aspect of instruction. Each student and each class is different, and you will have to modify, depending upon whom you have before you.

The best piece of advice worthy of repeating—not necessary from one of the renowned "experts," but from someone who is currently in the trenches, in their very own classroom—*Avoid getting frustrated if you tried something new and it did not work.* It seems simple enough, but sometimes hours of planning and a failed result can be exhausting. As you learn your student population, though, you will find ways to instruct that suit you and your students best.

So you can keep the educational instruction books on your shelf, but you can also feel successful, even when what the experts have prescribed is not quite right for you.

"THE FIRST SIX WEEKS"

On the eve of the first day of school, Ms. Engle sat at her faux-wood desk in her new leather chair and slowly spun herself around to observe the progress she had made in setting up her kindergarten classroom. Brights, pastels, words of wisdom, an art station, carpeted reading squares—the aesthetics pleased Ms. Engle, and she allowed herself to enjoy the fruits of her labor. About to begin her first year of teaching, Ms. Engle replayed the lessons she had learned as an undergraduate, the advice she had imbibed from those more experienced. She flipped through her binder, already filled with lesson plans for the month of September, quite satisfied by her type-A organization.

Wednesday morning rolled around, and Ms. Engle welcomed fifteen five- and six-year-olds. Overalls, oversized backpacks, bobbing ponytails, Velcro shoes, and expectant smiles filled the room. Ms. Engle took in the surreal scene; she had finally made it to where she had wanted to be for several years. "My own classroom," she thought, "I'm lucky."

"Welcome, everybody!" Ms. Engle beamed once the group was seated and settled.

Ms. Engle's teaching philosophy was not to waver from her six-week plan, part of the "responsive classroom" she intended to be absolutely perfect. In her undergraduate classes, many professors stressed the concept of the responsive classroom, a philosophy that urges the need for students to feel safe and emotionally fostered in order to succeed academically. Ms. Engle already planned to greet each student by name in the morning with a friendly smile, to give each student equal and positive reinforcement, and to establish a warm, inviting culture. Knowing the critical nature of the first six weeks, Ms. Engle put immense pressure on herself to set these standards immediately and firmly.

"Raise your hand if you have ever heard of a 'contract,'" Ms. Engle prompted the group.

Several students raised their hands, and Ms. Engle called on a boy with neatly gelled hair to explain.

"It is a thing that makes people agree with each other," he said, a bit nervously, looking around at his new classmates.

"Great!" Ms. Engle responded, "Well, today, we are going to make our very own Kindergarten Contract. That means we are going to write down some rules for how we can best be kind to one another and help each other learn!"

Ms. Engle used a three-foot-long piece of parchment paper to document the classroom rules.

"Who has an idea about how a good class works?" Ms. Engle looked kindly, eagerly at her students.

"We should say please and thank you!" one student blurted out.

"Very good," Ms. Engle said, "I'll write that one down! And, when we have an answer to a question, we should . . . ," Ms. Engle raised her hand in the air, modeling her expectations.

Ms. Engle and the kindergarteners worked on making a class contract for nearly forty-five minutes. Finally, after reviewing the contract, there was the exciting moment of "signing." Clad in canvas smocks, all fifteen students excitedly dipped their right hands in finger paint and made their permanent marks on the set of rules.

Ms. Engle patted herself on the back for this first step in responsive classroom set-up.

The rest of the first day was spent going over procedures—where to put backpacks, where to sit, how to stand for the Pledge of Allegiance, how to pick up and put away materials. All the while, Ms. Engle reminded everyone of their obligations to be kind to one another, to say "please" and "thank you."

By the end of the first week, Ms. Engle, self-assured in the flawlessness of her responsive classroom, confidently strode out of the building for a well-deserved weekend.

On Monday, Ms. Engle could not wait to see her students follow all of the procedures they had practiced the week prior, to see them implement all of those rules that they had come up with together.

However, Ms. Engle quickly realized that her spilled iced coffee was to be the least of her worries on this havoc-filled Monday.

Henry walked in and threw, not placed, his backpack (in the wrong spot); Monica, sleepy-eyed, cried when Ms. Engle asked her to stand for the Pledge of Allegiance, Catherine refused to partner with the boy next to her for a reading activity, and after snack time Ryan actually pushed one of his female classmates when she accidentally sat in his assigned seat.

Ms. Engle anxiously pulled out the class contract. "Ladies and gentleman, let's take a look at the way we behave in here," Ms. Engle's smile looked a bit manic.

She cleared her throat, "One: We are kind to one another. This means no pushing," Ms. Engle made eye contact with Ryan.

She went down the whole list of rules, and every child in the room seemed to stare at her absently. "Oh, God, what did I do wrong?" Ms. Engle thought, nervously.

The whole rest of the week Ms. Engle tried desperately to go back to the textbook definition of responsive classroom. Do this, do that, say this, say that. She felt she had lost her students. Her gentle reminders did nothing but elicit blank stares.

"I'm doing everything right, though." Ms. Engle pitied herself.

By the end of week two, Ms. Engle resigned to the failure of her responsive classroom. She made up her mind to try something entirely new the next week.

"I'll just have to be really stern, and yeah, I'll worry about how the students feel, but I need to lay down the law," Ms. Engle reasoned with herself.

And so, Ms. Engle really stood by her new stricter rules. During week three, Ms. Engle reprimanded students who did not follow procedures correctly. She was pleased at her progress as students gradually stopped acting out.

By the second month of school, Ms. Engle had earned the reputation of the "strict teacher," a title that kind of pleased the novice who felt she really had things under control. Students no longer threw their belongings or pushed one another, and this meant success to Ms. E.

As "pop-in" observations began, Ms. Engle felt confident that her principal would see the order she had established and would, consequently, be impressed. Ms. Engle's classroom still, outwardly, glowed with the same aesthetic appeal that it had on day one. The bulletin boards were pristine, the colors bright and inviting, the learning stations fully stocked and neatly maintained. "All is in order," Ms. Engle would think when she observed her own room.

One October morning, Ms. Engle's turn for a "pop-in" came. Ms. Engle went about her scheduled math lesson just as it was dictated in her digital lesson plans, and when Principal Kate left the room, she was certain she would receive an above-average review.

Ms. Engle showed up to her post-observation in a striped knee-length dress and a white cardigan. She rolled her shoulders down her back before entering the principal's office and held her head high before tapping lightly on the door.

"Come in."

Ms. E took a seat, and Principal Kate went through the expected pleasantries, and finally asked, "So, how do you think that lesson went?"

"Oh, it was great. Everyone was very attentive," Ms. Engle gloated a bit.

"Okay, I would agree that each student was very well behaved. But, Ms. Engle, you do realize that you are teaching five-year-olds. You did not smile once during that lesson, your arms were crossed, you did not address a single student by name. There was just no joy."

Ms. Engle's ego deflated as she let this truth settle in.

"Have you ever heard of 'responsive classroom?'" Principal Kate asked, handing Ms. Engle a book titled *The First Six Weeks*.

Reflection/Discussion Questions

1. How should Ms. Engle have approached her desired "responsive classroom?"
2. How can a teacher absorb an educational philosophy in a practical manner?
3. Was Ms. Engle correct to abandon the responsive classroom when it did not work immediately? How can a teacher create both a pleasant and structured environment?

"INTERMISSION"

Ms. Powers often treated her middle school classroom as if it was a stage. Her students sat attentively, looking up from their seats to the performance.

And Ms. Powers was really good at acting.

When an administrator would pass her room, you could hear that racket coming from the mezzanine.

Ms. Powers would dress up as characters; she would make loud, boisterous noises; she even answered her own questions.

On this day, Ms. Powers spoke of a novel and she never stopped, looking at students every now and then to remind them to "write this down." She loved gliding across that wide expanse at the front of *her* classroom. Some students loved watching their teacher's one-act plays. Some students became exhausted by Ms. Powers's own inner back-and-forth that they had no choice but to watch, sit back, and enjoy.

The whole notion of being in front of an audience every single day brought Ms. Powers back to her theater days.

She loved the concept of reinventing herself, fabricating small vignettes from her life, and watching her students respond in various senses of awe.

Admittedly, most of her stories were interesting—entertaining, even.

Others seemed a tad on the self-serving side.

Regardless, with a sold-out box office show every single day, and with an audience that was expected to behave, Ms. Powers was reliving her childhood dream with each and every line that defined her day's role.

And, as always, Ms. Powers was celebrated for her quirkiness and her whimsy.

Her supervisor entered the classroom. He had his gold-plated ticket to the next show, and it was about to begin, as the period 4 bell rang abruptly. Students filed in, took their seats, and awaited the opening act.

At this point, Ms. Powers did what she always did. Some students chuckled. Some students sat with earnestness. The rest just listened passively.

To Ms. Powers, this was the perfect show.

To her supervisor, he wanted his money back.

In their post-observation conference, Ms. Powers's supervisor had a *lot* of suggestions.

"You're like an actor on stage, did you know that?" The supervisor emphasized.

Ms. Powers blushed, "Yes; that's the whole point."

This exchange continued for the next thirty minutes. Ms. Powers had never received this sort of feedback, and as a result, the whole experience was jarring.

Soon, Ms. Powers attempted to put the supervisor's suggestions into action. She stood more on the sidelines and "made it less about her," using moments of time to get the students to become the actors on their own little stage.

To her surprise, little by little, the students needed her entertainment less and less.

Large questions were being posed to students—the types of questions that provoked students to *think*.

Students added to one another's responses, volleying feedback back and forth across the room—turning Ms. Powers's stage performance into an impromptu sporting event.

"It's hard to share the stage with someone, I know." Ms. Powers stood there in the murmur of her classroom chatter, with the words of her supervisor reverberating in her head.

"But you have to."

Ms. Powers stood there, as an audience member—no longer sharing the stage, but rather, walking off of it entirely.

Reflection/Discussion Questions

1. Why did Ms. Powers's supervisor want "his money back?" What exactly was so wrong with the manner in which Ms. Powers presented information?
2. What benefits can an animated teacher have for his or her students? What valuable lesson did Ms. Powers learn here?
3. After the post-observation conference with her supervisor, Ms. Powers adjusted her instruction. What might your own follow-up look like from the perspective of the teacher, and how would you inform the supervisor of any adjustments?

"BALANCING ACT"

In her first year teaching, Ms. Castro received study hall as her duty. When she shared her placement with her coworkers, they looked at her sympathetically, and quite frankly, rather smugly, relieved that they would not have the dreaded assignment.

Ms. Castro, who also taught U.S. history, thought she could use the time in study hall to catch up on grading or work on lesson plans. How difficult could a study hall really be? And, after getting the logistics of the duty solidified, Ms. Castro found that, like many other of the "warnings" she had received, the one about study hall was dismissible. She got to know teachers from other departments as well as students from other grade levels. On a bad day, she might have to confiscate a phone or a deck of cards, but even those incidents were few and far between. What Ms. Castro did not intend to gain from her duty were inadvertent insights from the students' idle chatter.

In Ms. Castro's several sections of U.S. history, she strove to challenge students while making sure her expectations were fair. She never really thought about checking in directly with students, but rather gauged her understanding of the level of engagement and difficulty in her class by assessing the grades students received, as well as their likeliness and eagerness to participate.

In study hall one afternoon, Ms. Castro overheard a student talking about a member of her department's class. She blamed the overhearing on the child's proximity, but in all honesty, her ears were open.

"Ms. Stein gave us two class periods to take notes. I literally was streaming Netflix for a period and a half and she had no idea. That class is an absolute joke."

"Okay, well that's better than Ms. Duran's class. She gave us literally twenty minutes to go through three sources and come up with a response. She's like, 'If you guys are going to talk to each other when I give you more time then you just have to get it done in a shorter frame,'" the girl speaking turned her face into a grimace when she switched over to her imitation.

The two students laughed in commiseration and continued working on another assignment.

Ms. Castro knew she should not have been eavesdropping on the conversation and knew, too, that she should take such commentary with a grain of salt. But, the Netflix confession sounded eerily truthful and the complaints about the limited time seemed genuine, too.

Ms. Castro thought about her own classes and wondered if she were more of a Ms. Stein or more of a Ms. Duran—she hoped neither, to be honest.

That day, Ms. Castro had planned an activity relating to Frederick Douglass's *Narrative*. As with any firsthand account, Ms. Castro wanted students to think about the narrator's reliability. In order to begin thinking about this concept, Ms. Castro asked three students to meet out in the hallway. When they came back into class, she wanted them to each tell the same story as if the events had happened to them, while only one person had truly experienced the events. Students in the class, after hearing all three stories, had to guess who the reliable narrator was. They then assessed what qualities make a person seem credible—perhaps the types of details they include, the chronology of events, their body language, and so on. The class then discussed a variety of factors that might make a narrator either reliable or unreliable. Ms. Castro thought everyone in the class seemed engaged and entertained and like they were really absorbing the concepts.

"See, no one is streaming Netflix in here. And no one is bored. And, I don't think anyone thinks they didn't have enough time for this."

Ms. Castro felt confident that her students were consistently engaged, but on days when the activities were not as hands on as the reliable narrator activity, she could not help but wonder if students were taking all they could out of her class. A few weeks after the eavesdropping incident, Ms. Castro asked students to fill out an anonymous survey. She used a simple online format and only included a few questions. She told students she wanted to touch base with them, that they could be honest and open in their feedback. She asked only a few, straightforward questions: Do you feel like you are always learning something useful during class time? What do you like most about the class? What do you like the least? Is the class fair? Do you feel challenged?

Ms. Castro really enjoyed her groups of students and felt confident that she had built a nice rapport with at least most of them, but she suddenly became really anxious for this anonymous feedback. She wondered if she had given the students too much power.

Ms. Castro skimmed the responses on the day they were due. For the most part, students responded in the way she had hoped they would. Most students claimed they felt engaged, liked the class, thought Ms. Castro was fair. However, about 20 percent of the responses confirmed Ms. Castro's initial fears. Some of the students, behind faceless screens, had been really cruel or maybe just really honest. The most troubling responses were the ones in which students professed that they were bored in Ms. Castro's class.

"I'm Ms. Stein," Ms. Castro berated herself.

Still worse were the students who claimed they did not think the class was fair, that Ms. Castro tailored activities for students who were outgoing and wanted to be the center of attention. Ms. Castro instantly thought back to the narrator activity, thinking, "I guess, yeah, only the most outgoing students would volunteer to be storytellers."

Ms. Castro entered her classroom the day after reading the anonymous feedback, and tried to act unaffected. But, now she was watching her every move. Was she being too subjective in her assignments? Was she boring students? She tried to use the criticism to better her teaching, but found herself "playing it safe" more often, trying not to alienate the shyer students in class.

Ms. Castro was not sure she had done herself any favors by surveying the students. She tried to block out the daily study hall critiques that floated in one ear and out the other. She noticed that students talked not only about Ms. Stein and Ms. Duran but about pretty much every teacher they came in contact with.

Ms. Castro wondered what they said about her.

Reflection/Discussion Questions

1. Should Ms. Castro have taken the two students' gossip seriously when she overheard their conversation? Should she have intervened in any way?
2. Was Ms. Castro correct in surveying students about different aspects of the course?
3. How could Ms. Castro have made the most of the survey results? Should she have shared the content with anyone else? How can a teacher be as objective as possible in creating lessons and activities for a class?

"COLUMBINE"

Projected onto the screen was the face of Kelly Fleming.

Mr. Pascale had students sit and stare at the large yearbook picture that emanated from the front of the classroom.

The virtually unknown girl sat in a light pink shirt. A look of solitude glossed over her face as she sat blankly toward the photographer.

And that was it.

Before students had the opportunity to inquire about this stranger, Mr. Pascale started with his introduction. As if he knew her personally, he spoke more and more about this Littleton resident.

Kelly Fleming was a young poet who spent most of her time in school daydreaming about what it would be like to be a famous writer. Her high school dreams were obvious to her teachers, even though she was the new girl in school.

That's why Kelly didn't know anyone, really. She found comfort in the school library during lunch. Being among those stacks of books made Kelly feel some sort of relief. She would write her free verse and think about how different Colorado was from the first fourteen years she spent in Phoenix. Things were new, but she was happy in her usual silence.

Mr. Pascale delivered Kelly's story to the students in his social studies classroom.

And, for whatever reason, the students in that classroom cared about Kelly and her story. They continued to listen.

"The school library is where Kelly Fleming would be shot, killing her," Mr. Pascale concluded. His somber tone resonated throughout the depths of the classroom.

Students sat silently.

In front of each student sat a folder with the Columbine High School seal emblazoned onto its cover. One student softly touched the seal's golden engraving before flipping its cover and beginning to read.

Evidence from the Jefferson County Police Department sat before their very eyes. Pictures of victims' clothing. Images from the crime scenes. Diary entries of the two shooters. It seemed so very *real*.

And that's because it was.

This was a *real* event, involving *real* people—like all of the history the students ever discussed in Mr. Pascale's classroom.

Students spoke in groups as Mr. Pascale circulated in the room.

And then he interrupted with the sound of a ringing phone, which would begin the live 9-1-1 call.

Some students looked physically horrified.

The pleading teacher's voice wavered in her recounting to the operator; she desperately panted and tried to catch her breath. In the faint distance, muffled sounds of gunshots could be heard. One thing was certain: Every student in that classroom, at that moment in time, internalized some piece of fear that was felt on the day by those on the other end of the phone line.

And then they started to put it all together—each segment of the timeline. Chronologically following the killers from beginning to brutal end.

In answering the lesson's essential questions, students were left with more inquiry than they were with answers. Because of this, they felt troubled. They wanted rationale. They needed to know *why*. Mr. Pascale, for once, had no absolute response for them.

In sifting through their folders, they found an image of the flower for which the town was named after—the columbine.

Students tried to make sense of all of the evidence provided to them. They tried to be mini-detectives, mini-lawyers, mini-psychologists, but still they were only left confused.

Mr. Pascale decided to continue their work into the next day of class.

Before the bell rang, one student raised his hand.

"I feel really terrible for Kelly Fleming," he added.

Mr. Pascale followed, "And that's the point. You'll never forget her name."

Reflection/Discussion Questions

1. How did Mr. Pascale's preparation contribute greatly to the execution of this lesson? What conscious decisions did he make along the way to continue in involving his students?
2. Why did Mr. Pascale use the class materials that he did? What sort of impact did this have, and how did it transform instruction on this day?
3. What should follow-up instruction look like for Mr. Pascale? How can he leave students with the answers that they might want?

"YOU'RE GOING TO HAVE TO PRODUCE DATA"

Ms. Oquente was the envy of many of her colleagues when her inclusive special education classroom turned out to have only five students enrolled. In Riverside School District, students between the ages of five and ten who required one-on-one paraprofessionals for severe learning disabilities were all grouped together. So, Ms. Oquente found herself with a group of five students: two five-year-olds, two seven-year-olds, and a ten-year-old.

The envy her classroom evoked was a misunderstanding, she thought, of how challenging it would be to make meaningful lessons and assessments for such a diverse population. Ms. Oquente was suddenly in a room with six adults and five children, and what many deemed a small classroom, felt more like a full house to this recent college graduate.

Ms. Oquente had begun the year by setting up her bulletin board with catchy phrases like "Dive into the School Year," with cutouts of fish displaying student names pasted on a blue backdrop. She wanted to make this classroom feel comfortable and welcoming.

Ms. Oquente received the list of student individual education programs and knew she was in for a challenging year. Some of her students were nonverbal, some had physical limitations, and all of them performed significantly below grade level.

Ms. Oquente was thrust into the school year under a new evaluation system, one that stressed the importance of several categories that Ms. Oquente thought seemed a bit unfair. "How am I supposed to have a student-run classroom?" Ms. Oquente asked.

She did her best, though. Sometimes a simple read-through of a children's book would take an hour, as Christopher often became restless and his one-on-one would have to walk him out of the room. Sometimes snack time became an ordeal when Ms. Oquente could not figure out what Elizabeth wanted to eat or drink.

Ms. Oquente was aware of the demands of the school district to produce tangible data of growth for each of the students in her course. And she did feel they were growing, but their victories were just vastly different from the victories of the "mainstream" kindergarten classroom down the hallway. None of Ms. Oquente's students were going to skip out of class reading full sentences by the month of June.

When benchmarks were due, Ms. Oquente became nervous.

She met with her supervisor and said, "I'm worried students won't meet the benchmarks that I've set for them. They are getting better with identifying their colors, they can sit still for longer periods of time, but I don't feel like I have anything concrete to show for it."

"Well, Ms. Oquente, you're going to have to produce data that we can turn in to the state. Measure for things like recognition of colors, numbers and words, measure for behavioral improvements, but make sure you have a starting point and an ending point and that the ending point shows improvement," Ms. Jahard forced a squinted smile at Ms. Oquente.

Ms. Oquente left the meeting even more stressed than when she had entered.

Ms. Oquente did want those end results to be better than the initial results, not for any state data but because she owed those students a productive year. Ms. Oquente would leave school each day exhausted, sometimes covered in food from snack-time mishaps, sometimes with bite marks that she lovingly dismissed as purely accidental. Her patience was awe inspiring, and her love for her students never wavered.

A typical class period included repetitive actions. Ms. Oquente would go through procedures such as sitting still for story time, identifying letters on specialized sound boards, and making requests to teachers in understandable ways.

By the time of the benchmark assessments, Ms. Oquente felt confident her students would show improvements. And they did. Christopher could focus on activities for 50 percent longer than when the school year began. Elizabeth could calmly signal when she was hungry, needed the restroom, or needed a break. The other students, too, had been able to identify accurately more letters and numbers than when the year had begun.

Ms. Oquente felt confident when she handed in her benchmark results.

When Ms. Jahard reviewed Ms. Oquente's data, the review showed that it technically did not meet the goals she had set. As a result, on the one-to-four evaluation system, Ms. Oquente received several twos.

"Your assessments don't yield enough growth, Ms. Oquente," Ms. Jahard said in their final meeting of the year, "Your overall score as a teacher is efficient, but next year, you need to work on better performances."

Part of Ms. Oquente was disappointed by the numerical results, but the other part of her felt pride when she looked at her group of five students and knew that no number could accurately portray the happiness each one of those students felt every time Ms. Oquente praised their very real progress.

Reflection/Discussion Questions

1. How much do assessments need to be tailored to an individual group of students?
2. Are standard evaluation systems always the best way to measure a teacher's performance?
3. How can Ms. Oquente foster growth in her classroom and please administration? Is this a feasible task?

"ALL BUT ONE"

"Have you ever seen *Wicked*, Mr. Damien?" Zoe wanted to know, as class ended one afternoon.

Zoe was the type of student to stay for a few moments after the bell rang to exchange small talk with Mr. Damien. He actually really enjoyed those innocent, easy moments. Zoe had just turned twelve, and for her birthday, her mother had filled her bedroom with green and purple balloons for Zoe to wake up to in the morning. Zoe knew right away that those balloons meant that she would be seeing *Wicked*, a play she had been *dying* to see for months.

"Yeah, so Mr. Damien, I wake up and I like can barely even see through all of the balloons and I just knew," Zoe practically squealed, "I just *knew* we were seeing *Wicked*. My mom is actually the best."

Mr. Damien was not particularly in the mood to entertain the conversation, but Zoe's genuine, innocent excitement was contagious.

"That's very exciting, Zoe. I hope it was a great show."

"Oh, it *was*. You would never believe how they do the lighting and so many of the characters are so different from what you might think and afterward I got two autographs. . ." Zoe elaborated on her fun-filled day until Mr. Damien gently directed her to her next class.

Mr. Damien, a few months into the school year, noticed that Zoe was often absent from class. After one week of straight absences, Zoe returned to class. She looked a little tired, and when Mr. Damien asked her if she had been able to complete any of the work he had sent home, she said she had not.

After class, he asked her, "Hey, Zo, do you think you'll have your part of the group work done by next week?"

"Uh, yeah, I'm going to try really hard, Mr. Damien." When Zoe looked down, Mr. Damien thought he might have seen a bald spot in the center of her hair.

No. Mr. Damien shrugged the thought from his mind.

"Uh, okay, Zoe, no worries if you can't, if you haven't been feeling well or anything. Just let me know so I can give you the extension, okay?"

Zoe nodded and went on her way.

Zoe was out for the rest of the week after that day. Mr. Damien went to check in with the nurse on Friday.

"Hey, Maria, is everything okay with Zoe Goldman? She's out *all* the time. She seems tired, too."

Maria looked at Mr. Damien, "Oy. So, okay. Zoe's parents have asked for confidentiality, which is why none of her teachers really know why she's out all the time. But, so she's still going for testing but they've started treating her for a really rare pediatric cancer. She'll be in and out often. Since her parents want everything to be private, you're able to enter any missing work as missing. They know the consequences. Zoe's guidance counselor should be reaching out to all of you soon."

The guidance counselor never did.

Mr. Damien felt like he had been punched in the gut. Poor Zoe. She was so tiny. It made him squirm to think of her hooked up to machines, fighting this private battle.

Though it seemed trivial in relation to her illness, Mr. Damien really was not sure what to do about Zoe's grades. She had still not returned to school, and when he entered incompletes for all of her missing work, she was suddenly failing seventh-grade reading.

When an e-mail went out for someone to complete home instruction for Zoe, Mr. Damien immediately signed up.

He went to Zoe's home and brought a variety of different assignments for her to work on. He nervously knocked on her door and entered a colossal foyer. "Whoa," Mr. Damien thought.

When Mr. Damien met Zoe at her kitchen table, he saw she was propped up with pillows in a wheelchair. Her hair looked different, and Mr. Damien wondered if it were a wig. Despite her fragile frame, Zoe looked delighted to see Mr. Damien and wanted to get to work right away.

As soon as Mr. Damien pulled out all of the missing work, he realized it was simply too much to tackle. He started with the easiest assignment, and by the time they were done, Zoe was visibly exhausted.

"Let's stop there for today, okay, Zo? We'll pick up next week."

When Zoe did not protest, Mr. Damien knew she must have been feeling pretty bad.

Mr. Damien soon realized that no amount of home-instruction lessons would actually bring Zoe to a passing grade for the marking period. He continued to meet with Zoe at home once a week until she was moved to permanent care in a local hospital.

Mr. Damien continued to visit Zoe at the hospital even when she could no longer lift up a pen to write, even when she no longer realized

Mr. Damien's presence. He would stay long after Zoe had fallen asleep, reading her pages from class assignments, reading her pages from some of his own favorite stories.

He visited every week until doctors made the decision to place Zoe in a hospice.

At the end of the marking period, Mr. Damien went through his grade book. He changed all of Zoe's grades to at least 65 percent. He knew she deserved to pass; he knew that sometimes objective numbers just do not reflect the truth behind a student.

Zoe never did make it back to Mr. Damien's class. She received incompletes in all of her classes that year. All but one.

When Mr. Damien appeared in that same colossal foyer to sit shivah for Zoe, he was greeted by Mrs. Goldman. She wrapped her arms around him, and whispered, "Thank you."

Reflection/Discussion Questions

1. What should Mr. Damien have done when he found out about the reason for Zoe's absences?
2. Was his flexibility in grading appropriate?
3. Should he have passed Zoe for the year? How can a teacher handle unique student circumstances when they arise?

"MORE THAN A FEW SECONDS"

Mrs. Rinkus was quick. Her life was accelerated and her classroom was much the same.

She had always been a gifted student, and because of this, she wanted to spend the rest of her professional days in a school building. In all honesty, Mrs. Rinkus relished the way she felt when she swiped in for the day—that sense of accomplishment and the yearning to get started.

Students entered the classroom as they always did.

Even through the morning announcements, Mrs. Rinkus gave students a directive—and pens were soon gliding on their slight pads of paper.

Her questioning was like a machine gun: rapid fire. One after the other. And Mrs. Rinkus's students sat, hoping to dodge each bullet.

Mrs. Rinkus's philosophy: this would keep students on their toes.

This also helped Mrs. Rinkus feel a sense of control.

Unfortunately, this made some students feel a sense of dread.

Students furiously wrote down each word as Mrs. Rinkus called on one student and another student and another student.

"Emily, what else do you see in this article?" Mrs. Rinkus chimed.

Emily sat for a moment. It's not that she wasn't paying attention, she just needed time *to think.*

A few seconds passed.

Mrs. Rinkus moved on to other students, who played Mrs. Rinkus's game quite well. She bounced from one student to the next. And they answered like good little soldiers.

The barrage of questioning did not cease. It usually never did.

Soon, Mrs. Rinkus was back to Emily.

Mrs. Rinkus was not giving up on Emily.

Emily felt like a victim being publicly shamed over and over again.

Mrs. Rinkus asked her question and a few seconds passed.

She moved on to other students—once again.

All of a sudden, Emily asked, almost pleaded for Mrs. Rinkus *to wait.* Mrs. Rinkus paused and returned to Emily.

The other students looked at Emily, not necessarily for her bravery or audacity, but mostly because her polite interruption halted the battalion from doing what it had always done.

So Mrs. Rinkus waited.

Emily finally shared her thoughts. Mrs. Rinkus thanked her, and she moved forward—because Mrs. Rinkus never ran out of her ammunition.

Mrs. Rinkus, although not always, waited more often after that.

Reflection/Discussion Questions

1. Why is "wait time" so important when we ask our students questions?
2. How else might Emily have handled this situation? Was the manner in which Emily interrupted class allowed in your classroom?
3. How might Mrs. Rinkus adjust her instruction moving forward? What should her classroom look like after this brief exchange with Emily?

FOUR
Professional Responsibilities

It is often when a beginning teacher starts their student-teaching experience that they realize that teaching is about one-half of what teachers actually do.

One morning, when Ms. Russell was in the midst of a partially finished do-now, homework-handing-in, one-million-student-questions kind of start to her day, her collaborative teacher reminded Ms. Russell, sternly, "You forgot to take attendance." Ms. Russell scrambled back to the classroom computer to enter the absences with a pile of student work under her arm and the sound of excited, unobserved student chatter behind her.

She thought, "Who would've thought taking attendance would feel like such a monumental task?"

But, teachers are known balancing-act experts, and while educating youth is the number-one priority, the number of additional responsibilities can sometimes be overwhelming. Taking attendance may seem the simplest task in maintaining accurate records, but try this undertaking when a group of thirty children is requesting your attention or when someone in the back of the room has a nosebleed or a major assignment is due the next day and no one wants to wait to ask questions about it.

Managing professional responsibilities, in addition to upholding a thoughtful, well-maintained classroom, is not an easy task, and the best way to take on these responsibilities is with foresight and preplanning, both of which take time to master. Maintaining up-to-date grade books and lesson plans is integral to a successful classroom, and teachers, aside from utilizing prep time, can take several actions to make the most of their days. Using independent do-now activities to keep students working while you are entering the attendance, updating participation grades, and so on, can be hugely helpful. Depending upon the age group with which you work, essay or test days are also great times to catch up on your own grading and planning. Any independent student work gives teachers a moment to get organized and get ahead—if done intelligently.

In addition to those more straightforward responsibilities, teachers can start to feel that they are an integral part of the school community by communicating with parents. While there will be individual students for whom you will need to reach out to parents, a good way to keep all parents abreast is through a quarterly newsletter or periodic e-mails about major happenings. This invites parents to ask questions and stay informed, and it often leads to a greater home-support system for both you and your students. Choose a system that is manageable for you, and do not give in to the pressure to follow the exact procedure that suits a colleague (because you will have a colleague who sends out daily e-mails).

As far as getting involved in the professional and local communities, you will find that the more activities you become a part of, the more your work begins to feel a lot less like work. While I may have rolled my eyes, initially, when I was asked to volunteer at the district's "Day Out," it has quickly become one of my favorite yearly activities. When teachers show up to community events, the experience is almost that of being a local celebrity, especially for teachers of younger students. Even the student who seems uninterested in your class will be delighted to see you spinning the candy wheel at the local carnival or running the 5K in town. These events bond teachers, students, and parents effortlessly, and they can really be a lot of fun.

Each teacher will have that one task that they habitually avoid. For Ms. Russell, she found reflection to be most menacing during her first year of teaching, and it often, unfortunately, did not receive the attention it deserved.

You will find that every person in the education field wants to offer you *their* advice; as with any advice, some is thoughtful and meaningful and should be utilized, while some you will listen to politely and think, "Well, that would never work for me." While ignoring the latter is perfectly understandable, write down those meaningful tips from other teachers, store them, visit them, attempt them in your work. Every so often, check in with yourself, either formally through journaling or just through an internal dialogue.

Are you following advice in a manageable way? Are you overwhelmed? Is your class running smoothly? Pause. Think about if you are doing your best work; and if you are, most importantly, make sure that you feel happy, fulfilled, and above water.

The more you reflect along the way; stay on top of your grading and planning (and attendance); get involved; remain open with communication; and continue to be the consummate professional, the easier teaching becomes. And, though these professional responsibilities are often referred to as something "extra" by many teachers and may not seem directly related to teaching, they certainly impact your stress level, as well as your confidence and comfort in the classroom.

So, the next time someone asks you to join their book club, to volunteer at their event, or to supervise a school dance, you may feel tempted to roll your eyes, but say yes. You will notice quickly how this singular decision can very easily impact your day-to-day experience.

"Re: Re: Re: Re:"

Mrs. Stryk was not happy.

So she decided to e-mail her daughter's teacher. Right that second.

It was a seventh-grade social studies classroom and Mr. Trign was reviewing the Holocaust. Mr. Trign stood at the podium in front of the classroom adorned with student work—stellar essays turned in the week before. Back-to-School Night was soon to come and Mr. Trign was currently in the process of decorating his classroom in a way that would impress the parent visitors in just a few days.

Students were to review primary documents related to World War II. Karen was always the quiet kid in class, very shy, and Mr. Trign had already heard about Karen's mother. As a result, he stayed away—almost out of fear of contact from the infamous parental unit.

On this day, Mr. Trign asked Karen to be quiet while he introduced the topic of concentration camps to students; after all, it is a critical piece of this unit of the curriculum.

Karen quieted herself and sat in silence for the remainder of the period.

Students then broke into groups and completed a task, as directed by Mr. Trign. The soft buzz of academic chatter emanated from the classroom. Students looked at a series of images related to the topics at hand. You could hear students' responses as they verbally reacted. The activity had the exact impact he wanted on students.

Karen sat in her group. Mr. Trign felt a sense of pride in knowing that his lesson plan had reached most of the class at that point.

In checking his e-mail immediately after school that day, Mr. Trign saw that he had received an e-mail from Karen's mother, finally. The e-mail had no subject line. She wrote in capital letters often and expressed her displeasure with Mr. Trign's handling of her daughter; in fact, Mrs. Stryk admonished Mr. Trign on the manner in which he disciplined her daughter.

Mr. Trign immediately spoke to his department colleagues, using Mrs. Stryk's e-mail as a joke of sorts—another token of the "crazy mom" at work again.

For the remaining days that week, Karen sat in her assigned seat, more quiet than usual. Mr. Trign could actually overhear some students asking Karen how she was doing, and although he could not hear Karen's response, he knew why she was not necessarily herself in room 403. He, however, moved forward with his lesson.

Karen spent her time doodling in her notebook, but made sure to nod her head every now and then to indicate to her teacher that she was paying attention.

Mr. Trign checked his e-mail that morning, at lunch, and even after school. During this time, Mr. Trign responded to the smattering of e-mails from Mrs. Stryk, defending his position and highlighting the classroom rules. Back and forth. Back and forth. With each click of the "send" button, Mr. Trign felt a pride in bolstering his side of the argument. He was somehow winning.

On the other end of the computer screen, Mrs. Stryk would talk out loud at her monitor, reading and rereading key sentences of her e-mail to her husband, awaiting any sort of revision advice. Every now and then, Mr. Stryk would have his wife make changes to language to make the e-mail that much more impactful. After all, this was a debate that *someone* had to win.

With each stroke of the keys, she would accentuate a sentence with a very purposeful exclamation point. She would kick in the CAPS LOCK to emphasize those points that needed to be stressed. Her daughter sat upstairs doing her homework. This passive-aggressive (or rather, at times, *aggressive*) game back and forth went on for a week.

Mr. Trign checked his e-mail first thing in the morning—in the quiet. Being an efficient taskmaster was Mr. Trign's admitted strength. He read through Mrs. Stryk's angry diatribe and sat in silence. His coffee mug to the right of his laptop. In the dark of his dining room table, the light from his computer's screen shone onto Mr. Trign's face.

This is certainly not the way he wanted to start his day. He took a sip of his coffee every now and then as he collected his thoughts—half because he was just waking up and the other half because he did not quite know how to respond. Mr. Trign drove to school and during the entire commute, he contemplated his response. He wavered between an attitudinal reply and a softer approach, but at this point, he was taking Mrs. Stryk's contortion of facts personally.

Good thing Mr. Trign had the first period off that day. He sat at his desk, paper-clipping classroom piles every now and then, multitasking as he always did. He then logged into his e-mail account, again.

Mr. Trign began typing back. He started out furiously:

Dear Mrs. Stryk,

. . . and then he stopped, he looked up from his desktop computer screen, and picked up the phone.

Reflection/Discussion Questions

1. A lot of things went wrong here, in looking from the outside into Mr. Trign's classroom. What do you think was the most difficult piece to watch?
2. In our experiences with parents, we will meet those who are not involved and those whom you may view as overinvolved. How do you deal with both similarly and/or differently? Which might you prefer and why?
3. How do we make parents a part of the student advocacy process so that the back-and-forth exchange never becomes personal? What can we do to ensure that this does not happen?

"CHANGE THAT"

"You should really have the agenda for the day displayed when students walk in. The objectives of the lesson also need to be visible every day. Student work groups should all have equal numbers of students. When students are talking among themselves, wait for them to be quiet before continuing with your instructions," Mr. Jackson, the high school principal, rattled off what seemed to be endless criticisms of Ms. Rowley's first observed lesson.

Of course, dispersed within these constructive critiques were many encouraging words. Mr. Jackson prided himself on his fairness, and the pride was well deserved. He could see and would objectively point out a lesson's flaws, while also acknowledging a teacher's best skills. His honesty remained an admirable quality even when Ms. Rowley could only absorb the criticism.

Ms. Rowley jotted down notes while Mr. Jackson discussed the content of the observed lesson. Ms. Rowley would make sure the agenda and daily objectives were displayed, rethink student groupings, and command attention before dictating directions. She planned to make these feasible adjustments as soon as she was back in the classroom.

As soon as she left the principal's office, Ms. Rowley put her loose-leaf notes from the meeting in the back of a folder in her bag. With ten minutes left of her prep time, she hustled into the copy room, and made a few last-minute printouts of vocabulary for the day's do-now. As the bell rang, her conversation with Mr. Jackson took a backseat to the group of teens present before her now.

Ms. Rowley began class in the same organized way she often did, with her do-now projected and a verbal announcement of the day's activities. The class ran quite efficiently. Ms. Rowley took attendance as students tinkered away on a vocabulary fill-in activity. Following this, groups of three and five students peer edited their latest writing assignment. Some individuals had questions, and Ms. Rowley spoke loudly enough for the whole class to hear the clarifications while groups continued working among themselves.

"Ms. Rowley, are we just checking the boxes or writing notes on the rubrics, too?" Sara asked with genuine interest.

"She just told us!" Patrick blurted back, with a mockingly facetious eye roll.

Ms. Rowley paused for a moment. "Mr. Jackson literally just told me to get everyone's attention before I give instructions," she thought, feeling almost like Big Brother was watching.

Ms. Rowley cleared her throat, "Okay, everyone. Ladies and gents. Please look up here."

Students looked up; the hum of student collaboration ceased. "I'll say this again, but everyone pay attention." Ms. Rowley smirked at Sara, "You are not only checking off the boxes on the rubric but also jotting down a brief rationale. If you are checking off an incomplete box for structure, for example, let your classmate know if they are missing a topic sentence, a concrete detail, etc. Any questions?"

No students raised their hands, and Ms. Rowley gave them the "okay" to get back to work. No one asked the same question again.

Ms. Rowley made a mental note of this result. Throughout the year, she did not have to think about pausing for a quiet room; the need for full-class attention became second nature.

Ms. Rowley adjusted her class appropriately. If the dynamic of a student group stopped working well, she changed it. If an assignment left students bewildered, she cleared up her expectations. When students seemed bored, she challenged them. When they seemed overwhelmed, she lightened the workload a bit.

Later in the year, Ms. Rowley's direct department supervisor, Mrs. Martin, observed her. Ms. Rowley's class was well behaved and worked busily during the observation.

Mrs. Martin told Ms. Rowley during the post-observation, "You know, Ms. Rowley, you don't have the daily objectives displayed anywhere in the class. How are students supposed to know why they're doing what they're doing? I went to a workshop the other day and leading researcher, So-and-So, said that our biggest fear as teachers should not be failure but mediocrity. Some small adjustments could really make a big difference in your classroom."

Ms. Rowley looked at Mrs. Martin with her head abuzz. Mediocrity. "Am I mediocre?" Ms. Rowley contemplated. The sting of the word rested visibly on Ms. Rowley's furrowed brow. Tempted to wipe Mrs. Martin's desk clear of her incense and self-help books, Ms. Rowley simply sat as stone faced as possible.

Reading her mood, Mrs. Martin continued, "And now, I'm not saying your class is mediocre. I just think, wow, what a great environment it could be if students were just one hundred and fifty percent clear on their expectations! And knew exactly what to expect every day."

Ms. Rowley responded with a nod and, begrudgingly, jotted down notes from her conversation with Mrs. Martin.

Fueled perhaps by anger but mostly by self-motivation, Ms. Rowley took her notes from the meeting and made Post-its. "Daily Agenda," she wrote on one, and stuck it on her computer screen. "Daily Objective," she wrote on another, and placed it adjacent to the first. "Mediocre," she wrote on a third and placed it, a bit more privately, on her desk calendar.

Ms. Rowley made changes immediately. Instead of simply displaying the do-now each class period, she had a visual of the daily agenda and the daily objective. Students both read the agenda and objectives and heard Ms. Rowley verbalize them. "I dare someone to ask these students if they know why they're completing the activity," Ms. Rowley thought.

Just as the full-class attention had become second nature to Ms. Rowley, so did the daily agenda and the daily objective. Eventually, she took the Post-its off of her computer screen; she had solidified her routine.

As the year progressed, Ms. Rowley did notice the lower frequency of clarification questions and general inquiries on assignments. Though her stubbornness disallowed her from admitting it, Mrs. Martin was at least partially to thank for that.

During April of that same year, Ms. Rowley was one of the last in her department to receive her third and final observation. She felt more confident in both herself and her students, but that "Mediocre" Post-it remained plastered on her desk calendar.

Without fail, Mr. Jackson came in on a spring afternoon to observe Ms. Rowley. Students were completing a close reading of a Z. Z. Packer short story and relating it the core text, J. D. Salinger's *The Catcher in the Rye*. Mr. Jackson clicked away on his laptop and made his rounds in the classroom. Students updated him on the assignment when he asked, and Ms. Rowley did her best to stay calm and go about business as usual.

On the day of the final post-observation, Ms. Rowley strode to Mr. Jackson's office. "Final critique of the year," she thought, "Bring it on."

Ms. Rowley fidgeted in her seat while she got out a pen and paper and looked up, keenly, at Mr. Jackson.

"Caroline," Mr. Jackson began, "Can I just start by saying I'm really proud of you? You know every year we take risks when we hire new teachers. You just don't know what you're getting." Mr. Jackson threw up his hands, "And a demo lesson and interview can only tell you so much." He put his hands down, "I saw potential in you, though, and you should know that I'm so happy you're a part of this district."

Ms. Rowley did not care what came next; a year of hard work, challenges and what felt like very little praise all felt justified in this moment.

Ms. Rowley looked down shyly but with gratitude, "Thank you for saying that."

60   *Chapter 4*

"As far as that lesson goes, good work. The objectives were clear, there was a visible agenda, students were busy working."

"Nice," Ms. Rowley thought, "Keep it coming."

"The groupings of students are still uneven," Mr. Jackson looked at Ms. Rowley, "Change that."

Ms. Rowley could not help but smirk. "You got it," she replied, letting her guard down a bit.

Ms. Rowley returned to her classroom. The desk calendar still had a hot pink Post-it that read, "Mediocre." She was tempted to cross it out, and write, "Human."

Reflection/Discussion Questions

1. How should a teacher prepare for a post-observation? Was Ms. Rowley prepared?
2. What should be the reaction from a teacher when he or she receives either praise or constructive criticism after an observation? Was Ms. Rowley's reaction appropriate in her observation with Mr. Jackson? With Mrs. Martin?
3. How should administrators frame their commentary when providing feedback after a lesson? How should a teacher make the most of post-observation feedback?

"TO WHOM IT MAY CONCERN"

Ms. Craft was an eleventh-grade social studies teacher. She was still fairly new, but no one could tell—an absolute natural in the classroom. And students loved her for it. In fact, she found solace in the classroom. She essentially felt more comfortable in front of a twenty-five-student class than she did in any social situation.

And history was Ms. Craft's life. Most affectionately, Ms. Craft would geek out over historical fiction in the privacy of her own one-bedroom apartment. She would Google political speeches—just for fun. Her college friends would invite her to new museum exhibits, and they would spend hours upon hours chatting about their mutual teaching duties. They would commiserate over the hours they spent on grading, paperwork, and lesson planning. Each of Ms. Craft's friends served as an exciting reminder of the culminating of their college degrees.

All their years in their bachelor's program talking incessantly about their future classrooms were finally a reality for each of them. Ms. Craft's exhausted excitement was evident in everything that she did. Teaching was her life, and she was proud of it; in fact, for her graduation gift, her mother purchased a piece of jewelry for her with the quintessential apple emblem. It sat dazzling around her neck.

At the end of the students' junior year, Ms. Craft purposefully adjusted curriculum to relevantly tackle the college search and the college-application process. Course content during the last month of school centered on the history of U.S. education. Many times, Ms. Craft would reference experiences from her own college years.

While she mostly shared these experiences in the context of this particular unit, Ms. Craft also found comfort in reliving her college years. She would cite examples from her dorm-room life to the hours upon hours of studying for finals in her own designated corner of the library. Specifically, she sat on the library's top floor, incidentally, among the social science stacks.

Students listened intently. Summer break was swiftly approaching, and they *still* sat listening intently.

Ms. Craft did a masterful job of interweaving education-history lessons with the actual exploration of students' own impending college search. Looking more closely at how a potential postsecondary education flourished in different regions of the country over time, Ms. Craft then highlighted key school programs—both locally and nationally.

She made sure to highlight the rationale for choosing her own college. A lot of it had to do with their history and education program. It was renowned in the state.

Students worked on investigating possible colleges for their own postsecondary plans. After all, Ms. Craft reiterated over and over to them that junior year was not too early to get themselves organized for the college years to come.

Lesson after lesson, students learned about how college programs and the college application process had evolved over time. It was now time for students to recognize their own role in these processes, as well.

Computer labs were reserved, helpful checklists were disseminated, and students began to work independently. The week before the school year ended, a student, Mallory, had a very relevant request of Ms. Craft: *Would you please write a letter of recommendation for me?*

Ms. Craft was immediately flattered. Mallory was not the best of students, and she was one of Ms. Craft's shyer kids. Mallory's love of history, though, was obvious. Ms. Craft got started on the letter that evening. She was excited to be a part of the process for Mallory. What was most powerful about this request was the intrinsic understanding by Ms. Craft that Mallory was one of those students who sat on the cusp of many colleges' acceptance lists—with high grades but mediocre test scores. The recommendation letter, undoubtedly, would tip her in one direction or the other.

Ms. Craft refused to recycle an old letter of recommendation that she wrote for a prior student and wrote it entirely from scratch. If only Mallory knew the efforts each keystroke would take (and how much easier it would be to simply replace one student's name with another). She read through the letter over and over again.

The final product read pretty beautifully.

Neatly folded and placed inside an envelope with the high school's insignia, Ms. Craft prepared how she would hand off the well-drafted page. She decided to keep Mallory after class the following day.

Wednesday's class was a lesson as usual. Students continued to be excited about the college process. Ms. Craft asked Mallory to stay after class.

As Ms. Craft sat at her desk, she pulled the pale yellow envelope from the top drawer of her desk. She presented the envelope to Mallory with pride, "This is for you."

Quite flatly, Mallory received the envelope and tucked it into a side pocket of her backpack. With a passing thank you, Mallory went on with her day. Ms. Craft went on with her day, her everyday schedule, moving from class to class, bell to bell.

Mallory's passing thank you resonated, reverberated even.

And Ms. Craft knew she would have to be okay with that.

Reflection/Discussion Questions

1. This anecdote portrays a very real view of the many extra tasks that we do as teachers. Is Mallory wrong in her approach? What should be the expectations of Mallory in this situation?
2. Ms. Craft has not written a letter of recommendation before, so this process is entirely new to her. How might she work through this process a little differently? What about her response to Mallory is admirable?
3. What other sorts of responsibilities must you be able to complete, and how do you manage these accordingly? How might other responsibilities differ than the one described in Ms. Craft's classroom?

"MASS DESTRUCTION"

Mr. Solowitz squinted at the sign-in sheet as he held it extended as far as his arm would reach. "Some of these parents need to come in when we work on penmanship," he thought. He, very meticulously, entered parent e-mail addresses in the "To" box and separated each with a semicolon. Mr. Solowitz muttered under his breath as he read through his "thank you" e-mail one final time. He selected "blind copy" and hit "send."

Mr. Solowitz applauded himself for creating a follow-up e-mail to thank each parent who came to Back-to-School Night. He anticipated that some would respond by saying, "Thank you for the thank you!" or, "It was great meeting you!" or, "I'm excited for my child to have you as his teacher!"

He received nothing of the sort.

A few failed-to-sends appeared in his inbox and one e-mail from Alexandra's mother with Alexandra's father copied on it.

It read: "Mr. Solowitz, Mr. Zach and I would like to meet with you as soon as possible to talk about ways to make sure Alexandra is successful in your class. Please give us times and dates that work for you. Best, Mrs. Schmidt-Zach."

Mr. Solowitz thought, "Well, I won't be sending one of those e-mails again. Helicopter parent on the horizon."

Mr. Solowitz ignored the e-mail until the following day. The more he thought about it, the more annoyed he became. "I sent a benign thank you e-mail, and now I'm being punished for it," he thought. For Mr. Solowitz, meeting with a parent meant he would have to tell his supervisor, and telling his supervisor anything during that first year of teaching, if he was being honest with himself, downright embarrassed him.

Mr. Solowitz logged into his e-mail at the end of the day, clicked on Mrs. Schmidt-Zach's response, looked to his right, to his left, and hit "delete."

"Maybe, she thought I was reaching out because I wanted to have a meeting, and she thought that was the appropriate response," Mr. Solowitz convinced himself, "I'm sure she won't reach out again."

A couple of weeks passed, and Mr. Solowitz forgot about the e-mail. Alexandra was quiet but smart, kept to herself but was respectful. She raised no red flags, and Mr. Solowitz conducted his class as usual.

Sipping his coffee while his students went to art class, Mr. Solowitz casually logged on to his computer to put in some lesson plans and read some e-mails.

His stomach sank when he noticed one from a sender with the last name "Schmidt-Zach."

Hesitantly, Mr. Solowitz opened the e-mail. Immediate dread ensued. In the copy section of the e-mail, he saw both the e-mail address of his direct supervisor and of his principal.

"Mr. Solowitz, I wrote to you after back-to-school night, and received no response. (She included her original e-mail as an addendum.) It is critical for Mr. Zach and me to meet with you because Alexandra has had bullying issues with another student in the class before. She sits close to this other student, and I would like to speak to you in person about this matter. —Mrs. Schmidt-Zach"

Mr. Solowitz put his coffee down, and went to see his supervisor. He tapped on her door and found her at her computer, freshly updated by Mrs. Schmidt-Zach's e-mail.

"What is this about, Steve?" she asked with genuine curiosity.

Solowitz came clean: "She e-mailed me after I sent a thank you e-mail, and I really wasn't expecting for anyone to respond like that. I didn't think she really wanted to meet. I thought maybe she was just someone who really likes to be involved in the school. I should've answered. I'm sorry. I didn't realize it was about a bullying issue."

Mr. Solowitz had to give Ms. Van Leven credit for her gracious response. "Well, you know you should've answered the e-mail the first time, but that's okay, we'll give Mrs. Zach a call later and set up a meeting."

"Mrs. Schmidt-Zach," Mr. Solowitz thought, but he said, "Thank you," and left the office.

When Mrs. Schmidt-Zach came in a few days later to meet with Mr. Solowitz and Ms. Van Leven, she brought her husband, Mr. Zach, and her youngest daughter. Mr. Solowitz sat down nervously, guiltily across from the family. Ms. Van Leven sat between them.

"So," Ms. Schmidt-Zach began, "We just really want to make you aware of some things that have happened in the past with Alex. Up until last year, she was really great friends with Kayla. They'd have play dates, sleepovers, the whole deal. But Kayla started saying things to Alex after she got new glasses. When Alex first told me, I thought, 'Okay, some gentle teasing. She'll get over it.' But, it got worse. Kayla started making clubs that excluded anyone who had a name that starts with 'A' then it was a club only for brunettes. It all sounds so silly, but Alex was devastated. They stopped being friends, and Alex tries to stay away from Kayla, but Kayla apparently makes comments to Alex in your class because she sits right next to her. She'll say, 'You're quiet today.' Or 'Nice shoes.' I just want you to be conscious of the whole situation because it's making Alex uncomfortable, and she sometimes doesn't want to come to school."

Mr. Solowitz wiped his cheeks with his hands and let out a breath, "I'm so sorry I didn't get back to you sooner. I'll make sure that I keep an eye on the situation, and if you want me to update you on anything, please reach out."

Alexandra's parents showed no signs of frustration with Mr. Solowitz and thanked him for meeting with them. Mr. Zach even said, "I know you only get a little bit of free time during the day, so we really appreciate this."

"I am a terrible person," Mr. Solowitz thought all the while.

When the parents left, Ms. Van Leven said to him, "See. Not so bad."

Mr. Solowitz considered himself lucky to have avoided what could have been a really tense situation. He vowed, from then on, to keep an eye on the bullying situation, to avoid mass communication, and to answer every e-mail that came in within twenty-four hours.

Reflection/Discussion Questions

1. How should Mr. Solowitz have reacted when he received the first e-mail from Mrs. Schmidt-Zach? What should he have done differently, if anything?
2. Did Mr. Solowitz respond appropriately to the second e-mail? What should he have done differently, if anything?
3. Did he learn any valuable lessons from the incident? Did he learn any negative behaviors from it?

"SECRET KEEPERS"

Hannah was a quirky kid. She had just entered high school and didn't quite know where she fit in. She liked weird facts, music, and artwork. She was the type of girl who kept a journal, and in this journal, Hannah kept poems and drawings throughout the meanderings of her day.

High school was a scary place. It was all new. The safety and comfort of middle school seemed just a distant memory.

That's why Hannah found the most security in the quiet of her art classroom—particularly after school.

Hannah's teacher, Mr. Nolan, was known to connect with the misfit students, and his classroom often served as a safe haven for those students who needed that place. Mr. Nolan had a gift of making course content and lessons not only relevant, but also enjoyable to the kids who needed the attention the most. Kids just like Hannah.

In Mr. Nolan's freshman art class, he decorated the classroom with student work. Portraits and introductory perspectives paintings were plastered from one wall to the next. Mr. Nolan reminded students of their worth and often referred to the artwork up on the perimeter; in fact, Mr. Nolan was celebrated as Teacher of the Year, even as a novice, third-year educator. Mr. Nolan was excited about education and valued students, not only as blooming artists, but also as developing people.

It was a Tuesday when Hannah had hit what seemed to be a breaking point. She remembered this Tuesday because it was her dog's birthday. She talked about her dog a lot in class. Rocky was a yellow Labrador and Mr. Nolan knew all about him. Mr. Nolan knew about all of his students' pets. He asked question after follow-up question, and because he cared, students talked.

Mr. Nolan was instrumental in coaxing Hannah into eating lunch in the cafeteria with the rest of her peers. He thought this sort of inclusion was important to a student like Hannah, and while he allowed her exclusivity in the quiet of the art room, Mr. Nolan slowly urged Hannah into sitting with several other art students in the cafeteria. Of course, this required Mr. Nolan to do some backdoor chats with those other art students, but eventually, this plan came to fruition. Hannah seemed really happy.

Cafeteria pizza, apparently, tastes much more savory among peers. Hannah preferred hers with extra cheese.

On this Tuesday, Hannah spent the after-school hour in the art room where Mr. Nolan circulated to help his students. Some students worked on lingering large projects; some students sat and worked on homework in other classes; some students just chatted about their days. Mr. Nolan would not allow gossip, however. He had a strong rule that students not talk about other students in his classroom. Students respected Mr. Nolan enough to only break this rule when they exited Mr. Nolan's classroom.

Hannah often remained after the rest of the students had already gone to their respective homes. Some had activities—extracurricular or otherwise; others just went home because it was an appropriate time to leave. Hannah lingered long enough to be continually kicked out by Mr. Nolan—kicked out only in the most passive, gentle of ways.

Mr. Nolan sat at his desk, grading schoolwork, his back to the doorway.

"All right, Hannah, time to pack up," Mr. Nolan shared with a sort of immediacy.

"Mr. Nolan, can I talk to you?" Hannah asked in an almost forced-quiet voice.

Mr. Nolan stopped what he was doing with urgency. He turned around to see what was wrong.

Hannah looked more somber than usual on this day, and once Mr. Nolan inquired, she poured out every single detail, sharing more with Mr. Nolan than he had even anticipated.

"I don't want to be here anymore," Hannah divulged mutely. She played with her strawberry blonde hair every now and then as she discussed the woes regarding her parents. It was a very similar story to those of many of Mr. Nolan's other students: Mom and Dad fighting with little to no time to tend to their children. This was something that Mr. Nolan almost *expected*.

Hannah, though, was talking about hurting herself and, in her very explanation, she was unclear. Still, Mr. Nolan took this threat seriously.

She pleaded with Mr. Nolan to not tell anyone. She was scared, and this would just make everything worse. Mr. Nolan promised to keep her secret and shared with Hannah how he had felt similar. Hannah, again, felt comfortable in trusting in Mr. Nolan as she sat engulfed in this very, very dark place.

Part of the deal: Mr. Nolan would keep Hannah's secret as long as she did not hurt herself. His bargaining came from a sweet, concerned place.

Hannah left for the day.

Mr. Nolan completed his remaining tasks, walked to the school parking lot, and drove away—just like any other day.

Hannah didn't hurt herself that night. Mr. Nolan was legitimately worried about Hannah, though. Many after-school sessions unfolded where Hannah reiterated some of the same sentiments from Tuesday.

It was Friday morning. Mr. Nolan walked to the second floor of the building to Ms. Rose's office. Under her nameplate, her position was emblazoned: *Principal*.

"Good morning, Gladys. Do you have a moment to talk?"

Reflection/Discussion Questions

1. At what point in Mr. Nolan's classroom was he the most negligent?
2. If such a situation occurs with a student like Hannah, what precise methodologies would you employ? How would you help Hannah?
3. At what point should Mr. Nolan reach out for help? When do we as teachers allow ourselves to keep secrets?

"A TRUE HONOR"

Mr. Simpson promised himself that he would get as involved as possible in his first year at Lewis Middle School. As many teachers soon learn, promises that you make to yourself in August sometimes feel daunting by the time the school year's responsibilities pile up in September and October. Mr. Simpson had not anticipated how much grading his eighth-grade science class would require, nor did he consider the amount of time he would spend planning, collaborating, and rethinking assessments. By the time the fall dance came around, Mr. Simpson was very much in need of a restful weekend.

The head of the dance committee approached Mr. Simpson, and asked, "Hey, do you want to sign up to chaperone the dance on Friday? It's a real treat," Ms. Franco elbowed Mr. Simpson, wide mouthed, showing her mock excitement.

"Oh, uh, I guess so," Mr. Simpson conceded, remembering the promise he had made to himself.

Ms. Franco was relieved after she expressed that he was the first person to say yes in a long line of coworkers.

Mr. Simpson almost immediately regretted his decision, but he went to the school dance with an open mind.

Upon entering the gymnasium filled with streamers, flashing lights, and punch bowls, Mr. Simpson was greeted by the pointing and squeals from several female and male students from his class.

"Ah, Mr. Simpson's here! Take a picture with us," a group of students surrounded Mr. Simpson and flashed several pictures. "Laura is going to be so mad she missed this," one of the girls in the photo claimed.

Mr. Simpson spent the rest of the night on the perimeter of the dance floor with the firm instructions to make sure the dancing stayed appropriate. He only had to intervene once, and by the time the dance concluded, Mr. Simpson was happy he had come.

Despite the busyness he felt in his first year teaching, Mr. Simpson continued to say yes to different opportunities in the community. When the school hosted a Saturday carnival, Mr. Simpson showed up and ran the coin toss. Again, students were thrilled when they saw him on the sunny weekend afternoon. Mr. Simpson made an appearance at each of the school plays, at the art show, and even at the robotics convention.

The principal of the school, Mr. Hartford, would joke with him when he spotted him at the events, "Are you trying to take my job?"

At the end of the school year, Mr. Simpson felt as though he had attended every event he could possibly fit into his schedule. One of Mr. Simpson's colleagues retired at the end of that school year.

Upon the retirement announcement, Mr. Hartford approached Mr. Simpson. He said, "Mr. Simpson, I've noticed how much time you've spent trying to get to know this community and your students both in and out of class. It says a lot about your character. I'm not sure if you know this or not, but Sandra used to serve on the anonymous board for the National Junior Honor Society, and we're going to need someone to take her spot. If you're up for the challenge, I would love to appoint you."

Mr. Simpson was grateful that Mr. Hartford would ask him to take on this duty, a responsibility that showed Mr. Hartford trusted Mr. Simpson's integrity and judgment.

"I would be honored," Mr. Simpson said, shaking Mr. Hartford's outreached hand.

Reflection/Discussion Questions

1. How can a new teacher get involved in the community without overloading his or her schedule? What might be a good place to start?
2. Did Mr. Simpson's appearances at the events earn him a spot on the school's honor society board?
3. What should a teacher hope to achieve in attending community and professional events?

"CHEESE SANDWICHES"

Ms. Haruta was new to teaching.
She was excited to start.

Her third graders were much different from the stuffed animals she would teach when she was once a youngster, though.

Fresh out of college, Ms. Haruta was enthusiastic. Her own classroom was set up with tables where groups of students worked together, much like the preschool where she worked throughout the summer. The students there referred to her as "Ms. Kelly."

Kelly Haruta felt more like a legitimate teacher as "Ms. Haruta."

In her free time, Ms. Haruta would read educational magazines that were sent to her home address.

Incidentally, Ms. Haruta had received these publications since her high school years, as a part of the Future Educators Club. And yes, she even served as president.

Ms. Haruta recognized that each day with her students would be different. With all of the different variables, she understood that each lesson would be no easy task. Her one constant was her lunch.

While she didn't have much of an appetite, Ms. Haruta drank plenty of water. And a sandwich. More specifically, American cheese on plain white bread. With a little dollop of mustard. Extra spicy.

Her lunch ritual was rather expected, almost identical from day to day.

Ms. Haruta would unwrap the contents of her brown paper bag. She would unveil the cheese sandwich from its aluminum foil exterior. She sat in the teacher's room with her fellow third-grade teachers.

Ms. Dieffen sat across from Ms. Haruta. Like typical teachers, everyone had their own assigned seats that rarely changed. Every now and then, if a substitute teacher was in, their lack of awareness to the predetermined seating arrangement often screwed up the order. Being too polite to correct the substitute, teachers would normally adjust themselves accordingly.

But usually, actually . . . always, Ms. Haruta sat across from Ms. Dieffen. By the second week of school, Ms. Dieffen would make constant commentary to the other teachers, joking about Ms. Haruta's taste in lunch.

"Cheese? Really? That's it? Her lunch is as boring as her." Ms. Dieffen would joke to her colleagues.

The other teachers chuckled in response, at times, but sat mostly in tolerance.

Ms. Haruta was perceptive enough to understand that Ms. Dieffen didn't like her as much as her seasoned team members. Regardless, Ms. Haruta bit into her sandwich—corners first.

Sometimes she left her crust.

In the teacher's lounge, Ms. Haruta would exchange ideas about lessons with her veteran mentors and ask questions. A lot of questions.

Ms. Dieffen and her colleagues helped to answer Ms. Haruta's inquiries—often about lesson ideas and classroom management suggestions.

Ms. Dieffen avoided the teacher's lounge every now and then and instead ate her lunch in her own classroom.

Ms. Haruta never missed school, though, and she always sat in her designated seat.

"She's here again. With her stupid cheese sandwich. I can't stand her," Ms. Dieffen would share with her fellow veterans in privacy.

Only this time, Ms. Haruta overheard Ms. Dieffen's diatribe as she approached the doorway.

She ate her cheese sandwich alone that day.

Reflection/Discussion Questions

1. We won't always work with people we like and enjoy. At times, just as in any workplace, there may be people who annoy us. How do you work with those people appropriately and professionally?
2. What was your biggest issue with regard to Ms. Dieffen's behavior? What about the rest of Ms. Haruta's colleagues? How could this have been addressed differently?
3. Ms. Haruta is obviously in an interesting predicament. She is a new teacher and wants to form relationships with her colleagues. She also recognizes that there is some tension. How does Ms. Haruta navigate professionally from here?

"THE EXPERT IN ANYTHING WAS ONCE A BEGINNER"

Back-to-School Night. The digital marquee outside of HHS displayed the four dreaded words in a loop each September morning as Mr. Grant pulled into his assigned parking spot.

Up until this last Thursday of the month, he was able to put the event on the back burner, focus on getting acquainted with his first class of students, and pretend the school-related nightmares were merely coincidental. But, tonight, Mr. Grant was going to meet his first set of parents, many of whom had children his own age. One part of him felt those first-day-of-school butterflies that many teachers lovingly experience, and the other part of him felt genuinely fearful. He wondered, nervously, if parents would like him, if they would take him seriously, and, most importantly, if they would leave feeling confident that their children were getting a great education.

So, on this last Thursday of the month, Mr. Grant worked from 7 a.m. until the 7 p.m. parental arrivals. His classroom was impeccable; he had prepared a brief slideshow, had rehearsed in front of very supportive, veteran coworkers. He even declined the invite for a pre–Back-to-School Night dinner with his colleagues.

"Just be yourself. Greet the parents in the same way you greet your students. Pretend they're just another audience of teens," Mr. Grant looked at himself in the faculty bathroom mirror, silently pep-talking himself while smoothing his collared button-down.

He took a deep breath as the first bell of the night signaled the start of a pressure-filled meet-and-greet.

Infinite "Hellos," "Nice to Meet Yous," and "I'm Mr. Grants" later, and the second bell signaled the beginning of his presentation.

Parents began their mock do-now, and wrote down an interesting fact about their child for Mr. Grant to read later on. They flipped through a sample syllabus while Mr. Grant began his much-awaited introduction. With only a seven-minute time frame, Mr. Grant explained, as thoroughly as possible, his expectations for the school year, his plans for his students, and his excitement in starting his career at HHS. Without fail, the third bell of the night sounded, and parents filed out.

"Well, that was pretty painless," Mr. Grant thought as his nerves eased and his confidence rose in anticipation of the next set of parents.

The night flowed easily. Mr. Grant shook hands, smiled, shared his classroom with parents, and felt as though he might actually get a good night's sleep that night.

The second-to-last bell of the evening sounded, and it was time for period 9, one of Mr. Grant's AP chemistry classes. As parents trickled down the hallway, Mr. Grant noticed two mothers eyeing one of their children's schedules. This relatively common look of back-to-school night confusion was nothing to worry about—a completely understandable occurrence for anyone navigating a large and unfamiliar building. Mr. Grant thought little of it, until it was apparent that there was not confusion regarding the location of a classroom or the rotation of the child's schedule.

"Oh, God! Matthew has Mr. Grant. You know he's twenty-two years old, straight out of college, fresh-paint teacher, doubt he knows what he's doing," Flustered Mom 1 said, loudly, to Mom 2.

When Mom 2 realized Matthew's schedule indicated the classroom directly in front of her, her face turned a bright shade of crimson, and she slunk, guiltily, into Period 9 AP chem, giving Mr. Grant a sheepish close-mouthed smile and a wave. Mom 1 continued on, entirely oblivious of the anonymous insult she had just issued.

Mr. Grant's earlier nerves not only returned, they multiplied. He had finally convinced himself that his fears were ridiculous. He was qualified, dedicated. Why would a parent not want him as their child's teacher? But, that insecurity had been fueled again, and he nearly forgot what he was even supposed to say to this final group of parents.

Mr. Grant stammered through his presentation. He had four full minutes remaining when he was done with his spiel and asked if parents had any questions. They did not.

Just the sound of pages of syllabi flipping until the merciless clock finally ran out. Mr. Grant thanked everyone for attending.

Mr. Grant could not quite pinpoint his emotions. He thought maybe he felt angry at the unwarranted accusation from Mom 1. He thought maybe he should have addressed his age and his greenness in his introduction. Unsure, regretful, and quite hurt, he controlled the fragility of his tear ducts while seeing parents to the door.

When Mr. Grant noticed Mom 2 lingering for a moment, his nerves again multiplied.

"I actually just went back to school four years ago and got certified to teach. I'm at the middle school teaching fourth grade now. It's not easy work!" Mom 2 said to him with a true air of camaraderie.

"Yeah, it's my first year, and I'm getting used to it, but it is definitely difficult! I'm enjoying it, though, and Matthew has really been such a great student to have in class," Mr. Grant replied, thankfully.

Mom 2 put her hand on Mr. Grant's shoulder, "It's going to be a great year," she said, with palpable sympathy and understanding.

Mr. Grant packed up for the night, and thought he would soon put the whole incident behind him.

He could not have foreseen that he would not soon forget the approval Mom 2 had given him that night. Not when a hall monitor stopped him because he looked so much like a student, not when a substitute for his special education collaborator did not believe he was the real teacher in the room, not when disgruntled coworkers made jabs at his youth, and not when he, himself, felt the weight of being a novice.

Reflection/Discussion Questions

1. How should a new teacher prepare for Back-to-School Night and other parental interactions?
2. How should a teacher react if a parent questions his or her credibility? Was Mr. Grant's reaction appropriate?
3. Is it unprofessional for a teacher to appear nervous or to be impacted by external factors when giving a formal or informal presentation?

"HASHTAGS AND FRIEND REQUESTS"

It was her friend's twenty-fourth birthday party. Ms. Madag had been friends with Lindsay since high school. Truly, it would be a night to remember. The evening would be especially nice as everyone in "the group" had decent jobs that paid decently. It was to be a big event.

Ms. Madag jetted out of the school building and hopped into her Volkswagen. Just a thirty-minute commute and she would be home to commence a carefully planned nap.

Friday, 3:18 p.m.—Status update: Annoying students on a Friday. Can't wait to sleep.

Ms. Madag woke up to a flurry of text messages from Lindsay and everyone else who would be attending the night's activities. After brushing her cat off of her bed, she picked up her cellular mobile device to respond, reply, and repeat.

Her outfit was already laid out on the living room couch—a purple dress, newly purchased, with silver-hoop earrings. And the bargain she got for her new shoes was pretty impressive.

Friday, 6:02 p.m.—Status update: New outfit for the big night! Who's ready to party?

The cab picked up the girls; Ms. Madag could not wait. The girls had their birthday sashes on, snapping pictures, blasting music, and enjoying what would be a much-needed weekend. In the backseat of the cab, the girls talked about their weeks—most of the chatter veered into relief that the week was *finally* over. The cab stopped, and the ladies piled out one by one.

The evening started out with shots of vodka. There was no other way to commence any Lindsay-celebration than with a bottle of semi-expensive vodka. The evening already began with hooting that had the entire bar looking in their direction, and perhaps that was the point of all the jovial commotion in the first place.

Friday, 8:44 p.m.—Status update: My students drive me to drink! Five vodka tonics in already!

The pictures posted were fun. The group of six girls huddled around in different configurations, each tilting her head ever so slightly in order to maximize camera angles and proper lighting. As a collective group, each girl's individual attention to her pose contributed greatly to the final product of each shot. Of course, if one girl's eyes were closed or looking in the wrong direction, they were either cropped from the photograph—or even better—posted with an even more clever caption than before. After all, documenting the mess made things *that much more fun.*

The entire night, each girl drank, hollered, and subsequently looked down at their iPhones. With each swipe and each tap, the girls shared their grandiose event with the entire world—each photograph more interesting and beautiful than the last.

Friday, 11:18 p.m.—Status update: SOOOO WASTED%~! TIME 4 ANOTHER DRNNK!

The dancing continued. And the music grew louder and louder. Glassful upon glassful was imbibed, and the night became more fun than any of the girls could even post about. They were, still, fixated on finding a way to translate the pandemonium of Lindsay's birthday to each of their friends and followers. Videos of booming music, strobe lights, giddy shouts in the near distance, one after the other. Their digital walls were streaming with the most entertaining data. At one point, the girls proclaim, in almost exact synchronicity, a happy birthday to Lindsay. Lindsay, by midnight, could not enunciate a complete sentence without falling (both literally and figuratively) into a slurred mess.

Saturday, 12:43 a.m.—Status update: Lindsay can't even stand up! Look atT her! HAhaa

The status updates ended after that. Lindsay's birthday was now nothing more than a memory—a well-documented one.

Monday, 1:31 p.m.—Look at my student's work! Grammar is a lost skill in our country!

Ms. Madag's cell phone sat always at her side. The need for instant access encouraged her oversharing of any and all events. To her friends, it was the inside joke, something that they would joke about from one post to the next.

The school bell rang and Monday's workday was officially over. Ms. Madag was called to the principal's office.

Ms. Madag walked in and her stomach sank.

There sat Mr. Rewsnok, holding an image of Ms. Madag with a beer bottle in one hand and a joint in the other.

Reflection/Discussion Questions

1. As teachers, we serve as professionals twenty-four hours a day. On the schoolhouse property and off. How could Ms. Madag have treated these circumstances differently?
2. What was most egregious about Ms. Madag's behavior on that fateful Friday night?
3. Ms. Madag wakes up on Saturday morning. How might she have rectified the situations from the previous evening?

"BEWARE THE IDES OF MARCH"

A standard public school year has ten months. Until Miss Jordan became a teacher, she assumed that each year was its own mutually exclusive entity. She pictured guidance counselors, administrators, and teachers using those elusive summer months to prepare for the upcoming year, while the current year was all about, well, the current year. However, the amount of planning required for yearly events including academic schedules, sporting events, testing, graduation, and so on is so daunting that the administration really begins planning the next year, at least in Miss Jordan's district, by the month of February.

So, in March, Miss Jordan received an e-mail regarding a few opportunities for what would be (contract pending) her second year in the district. Miss Jordan read through the stipend-ed offerings: Head Cheerleading Coach, Winter Track and Field Assistant Coach, Junior Class Advisor. "No, no, no," she thought, while scrolling through the list. The last description on the e-mail caught Miss Jordan's attention. It was not for an extracurricular activity but for an opportunity for a teacher to take on a sixth class in place of a prep period. The class would be a support for students from the school's Program for Students with Additional Assistance (PSAA). The program provides a safe haven for any students who have intense anxiety or depression, are going through difficult situations at home, or simply want a comfortable space to talk about everyday stresses. Miss Jordan worked closely with several PSAA students in her eighth-grade algebra class and knew she could be a really great addition to the program.

She responded to the principal's e-mail with a brief cover letter, her résumé, and a short blurb stating, "Please see attached. I'd love to become a part of this program!" She hit send, and knowing many other teachers would jump at the opportunity for a 1/6 pay increase, she did not get her hopes up too high.

Miss Jordan did not know the staff of the PSAA program exceptionally well. Miss Jordan had met with one of the PSAA counselors about one particular student, Michael, who had raised several alarms; the student's behavior remained stagnant, which Miss Jordan thought frustrated both her and this PSAA counselor alike. Aside from those interactions, she knew the PSAA counselors on a mostly smile-and-wave kind of basis. Miss Jordan was aware that Mr. Green would meet with the PSAA staff before deciding on the right teacher for the job. She was hopeful the staff would put in a good word.

Miss Jordan got back to her regular routine. Testing season was around the corner, and she spent a lot of class time going over sample problems, reviewing and repeating.

A few days after submitting her application, Miss Jordan received an e-mail from Mr. Green asking her to meet in his office to discuss the PSAA position. Miss Jordan got butterflies in her stomach. "They must have picked me," she went into Mr. Green's office beaming.

"Miss Jordan, take a seat, please," Mr. Green looked more serious than usual.

"So," Mr. Green let out a slightly exasperated sigh, "I don't even really know how to say this."

Miss Jordan's butterflies turned into weakened knees. "My God, what is he going to say?"

"So, it isn't policy to even tell you what I'm about to tell you, but, Miss Jordan, I have a great relationship with you, I trust you, and I want to be honest with you."

"What is happening?" Miss Jordan's mind went wild.

"I met with Ms. Mundane from PSAA and Mr. Juno, head of Special Services, to discuss the 1/6 class for next year. I mentioned your name as a potential teacher. And, Miss Jordan, Ms. Mundane told us that you have 'boundary issues,' that you have students' phone numbers and you text them about non-school-related happenings."

"What in the actual—" Miss Jordan's inner dialogue became violent.

Miss Jordan began to shake. "I just don't know why someone would say that, Paul. I honestly don't even have a single child's phone number. Why would I?! I would never text a student. The students don't know my number, either. This is all just so crazy. Can I please go talk to Ms. Mundane about this? I want to know why on earth she would say something like that to, no offense, but my boss of all people," Miss Jordan could not hide her hurt frustration.

"No, no, Miss Jordan, I was not even supposed to tell you what happened in that meeting. But, when another teacher brings up an allegation like that, I have to investigate. Please don't be upset. I believe you. I trust you. I just, for legal reasons, needed to hear you say that. I'm going to call in Ms. Mundane tomorrow and ask her to elaborate on her brash statement. I will get back to you."

Miss Jordan, who prided herself on her ability to stay rational, to stay reasonable, found herself walking in the direction of Ms. Mundane's office. Her heart beat uncontrollably, her jaw was clenched tightly, she wanted to know why, why Ms. Mundane had blatantly lied about her to her superiors. It was an act of disloyalty Miss Jordan could have never foreseen, and her generally coy demeanor was trumped by her thirst for explanation and justice. As Miss Jordan stormed down the hallway and came closer to the PSAA office, she heard that ever-pestering inner voice of hers: "Relax. It's not worth it."

Miss Jordan walked straight past the PSAA office and into her car. She called her mom on her way home, needing an outlet. To this day, she thinks that conversation might be the angriest outburst she has ever spewed. Her mother tried to calm her, told her not to take any irrational actions, and assured her, as all good mothers do, that she was proud of her and that everything would be okay.

Miss Jordan did not sleep that night. Going against protocol, the next day she went straight to Mr. Green's office and demanded to hear Ms. Mundane's response to his inquiries. "I need you to ask her or I have to," Miss Jordan kept her voice steady, firm, and as professional as possible. Mr. Green must have seen the dark circles under eyes, the shaking hands, and he agreed to talk to Ms. Mundane first thing in the morning.

Miss Jordan checked back in with Mr. Green at the end of the day. He closed his office door, and sat behind his desk.

"Okay, so," he began, "I spoke to Ms. Mundane. I asked, 'Who told you Jordan texts students?' She kind of waved her hand and said, 'Oh, I don't know. I don't remember. One of the PSAA kids I think.' I told her this was unacceptable. I said, 'I need a solid answer about where this information came from. You can't blindly make an accusation like that.' Ms. Mundane came back to me later in the day and told me Michael told her in group one time that 'he got your digits.' Okay, now Miss Jordan, before you respond, on a credibility scale, Michael is here" Mr. Green placed a flattened hand below his desk, "Ms. Mundane is here," he raised his hand to desk level, "And, Miss Jordan, you are here," Mr. Green raised his hand above his head.

He continued, "I don't know why Ms. Mundane would bring useless information into a meeting like that. It is not going to impact our consideration of you for the 1/6 position. Now, go get some rest."

Miss Jordan left for the day, infuriated still but remembering her position on Mr. Green's pantomimed scale.

She, over time, let the anger slip away, and finished out her year with dignity. Though the smile-and-wave basis turned into more of an I-know-what-you-did-smirk-and-wave.

Miss Jordan did not receive the 1/6 position.

Reflection/Discussion Questions

1. How should Miss Jordan have reacted when Mr. Green told her about the PSAA meeting?
2. Should Miss Jordan have confronted Ms. Mundane? Should Miss Jordan have gone to Mr. Green for a second time without being prompted?
3. Was there anything Miss Jordan could have done to avoid the situation? How should a teacher react if a rumor or false allegation surfaces?

Final Thoughts

FINAL WORDS FROM A TEACHER...

I am not surprised to find teaching at the top of lists like "Most Rewarding Jobs" and "Most Meaningful Careers." After all, stress and reward often go hand in hand. Teaching is a true balancing act of preparation, planning, classroom management, event attending, and much more. And while the weight of teaching can sometimes feel overwhelming, the joys always outweigh the day-to-day trials.

At the last high school graduation I attended, I watched as my first class of sophomores strode to the classic sound of "Pomp and Circumstance" toward a stage of gown-clad administrators. I watched as 250 newly minted young adults, some teary-eyed, some elated, took that symbolic step toward the future.

I thought back to when I had first met many of them. They had all been physically smaller, many less confident, and now they stood at this monumental ceremony, ready for college, for internships, for new friendships. I doubt any of them were thinking of me as they turned their tassels from right to left, but I looked at them and knew that the experiences we had shared had played a role in this moment. I clapped as the last student received his diploma, and not an obligatory clap. I knew how many people had come together to make this group of people successful, and whether they realized it or not, I was clapping not just for the students but for every parent who spent tireless hours helping with homework, carpooling, and attending sporting events, and for every teacher who graded countless tests, quizzes, wrote letters of recommendation, and shared, truly, in the joy of their students' accomplishments.

As the seniors exited the auditorium, I thought, "It isn't easy, but it's worth it."

FINAL WORDS FROM A SCHOOL ADMINISTRATOR...

On graduation day, I have the opportunity to look upon the vast group of seniors—all suited and shiny for their last united, singular event together.

From my perspective on that stage, I can also see dots of those students' teachers scattered throughout the onlooking audience.

I remember, as a teacher, attending graduation and finding the weight of the whole event to be somewhat burdensome. I found myself, as a new teacher, being almost envious of the journey for these kids that went far too quickly for me—the first days of college, the horror-roommate stories, first-career interviews, and then all of those beautiful moments that fall into place once their education is over.

The envy has dissipated tremendously.

I now sit with pride that the collective effort of all of those people in the same auditorium comes to a shared culmination.

Regardless of any issues or any misunderstandings, this large group of seventeen- and eighteen-year-olds is about to embark on a whirlwind of a lifetime that they know absolutely nothing about. Each student has either faked their way, coasted, or sifted through pages upon pages of work to get to their very seats. And on this day, it would all end. Or it would all begin.

I see a student in that group who barely made it.

I see a student in that group who lost her father just a month ago.

I see a student in that group who found their way.

I see a student in that group who felt valued, *finally*, by someone else who sat in that same auditorium.

I get teary on graduation day because, while I know that the pages read have been important, I realize again every year that it is the teachers who *cared*, it is the teachers who stopped to say "hello" to a student in the hallway, it is the teachers who reminded students that they mattered— those were the most powerful lessons of all.

Perhaps this is the last time that they feel this sense of worth, as we release their fledgling selves into the large landscape beyond our tidy microcosm; but regardless, they felt *something* along the way.

They felt something along the way because of the people sitting in that audience.

When we truly teach, we go "to school," not "to work."

Make your kids believe that, and they'll do the same.

About the Authors

Dennis M. Fare, MEd — School Administrator

Dennis M. Fare is currently an assistant superintendent for the Mahwah Township Public Schools in New Jersey, where he oversees the hiring and evaluation of all nontenured and novice teachers. He has also served as supervisor of English language arts for the district. After teaching English for many years in an urban district, as well as English education, literacy education, and school administration and leadership at the college level, he knows the importance of the preparation of new teachers to the vocation.

Dennis holds a BA in English writing and an MEd in English education from Marist College in Poughkeepsie, New York. He also holds supervisor, principal, and superintendent certifications. Currently, through the University of Arkansas, Dennis is a doctoral candidate through their Human Resources and Workforce Development program.

Allison Coyle—Teacher

Allison Coyle is an English teacher for the Mahwah (NJ) Public Schools. She has been an active curriculum developer for the English Department, working to implement a variety of best practices, while maintaining and fostering an appreciation for classic literature. She has a bachelor's degree in English literature and secondary education from Marist College and currently attends Rutgers University–Newark (NJ), where she is pursuing a master's degree in English with a concentration in women's and gender studies.

www.ingramcontent.com/pod-product-compliance
Lightning Source LLC
Chambersburg PA
CBHW020753230426
43665CB00009B/582